A STUDENT'S GUIDE TO A MEANINGFUL CAREER

Choices, Education, and Opportunities

Vickie Ann McCoy

cognella® | ACADEMIC PUBLISHING

Bassim Hamadeh, CEO and Publisher
Kassie Graves, Acquisitions Editor
Berenice Quirino, Associate Production Editor
Miguel Macias, Senior Graphic Designer
Alexa Lucido, Licensing Associate
Don Kesner, Interior Designer
Natalie Piccotti, Senior Marketing Manager
Kassie Graves, Director of Acquisitions and Sales
Jamie Giganti, Senior Managing Editor

Cover image copyright © 2015 iStockphoto LP/andresr.

Printed in the United States of America

ISBN: 978-1-5165-1543-1 (pbk)

A STUDENT'S GUIDE TO A MEANINGFUL CAREER

Choices, Education, and Opportunities

DEDICATION

This book is dedicated with appreciation and affection to three people who were instrumental on my journey when I was where you are now.

When I was a student at Keyport High School (KHS) in New Jersey, I had no intention of attending college. I planned to get my diploma and head to work as so many of us did at that time and in that town. My guidance counselor, Mr. George DeBonis, asked me to just take the PSAT because all students at KHS needed to take it. He then took me aside and convinced me to just take the SAT, offering to pay for it himself if necessary, and hooking me in with a passionate speech about full scholarships that included room and board. He lured me step by step into a promising new future.

When I was a first-year undergraduate college student (on the aforementioned full scholarship), I received a work-study position in the Life, Career, and Advising Center (LCAC) at Monmouth College (now University) in New Jersey. I was a 19-year-old undeclared student who was most interested in my housing concerns, my new friends, and the beach a mile up the road. It suffices to say that academics were not at the top of my list, and career planning was not even on my radar.

The Dean of Student Life and Director of the LCAC, Mary Abate, saw something in me that I did not see in myself, and she advocated on my behalf and offered me many opportunities to grow.

A few years later, when I returned to Monmouth for graduate studies, the Director of Career Planning and Placement, William Hill, offered me a graduate assistantship. Again, he had greater confidence in my abilities than I did and taught me a great deal about that office. Though not cited directly, his ideas influence the tone and direction of this work.

So thank you, George DeBonis, Mary Abate, and William Hill for believing in me and showing me that, like you, part of my career path is helping others find theirs. You made a difference and I think of you when I pay it forward.

THE COGNELLA SERIES ON STUDENT SUCCESS

Student success isn't always measured in straight As.

Many students arrive at college believing that if they study hard and earn top grades, their higher education experience will be a success. Few recognize that some of their greatest learning opportunities will take place outside the classroom. Learning how to manage stress, navigate new relationships, or put together a budget can be just as important as acing a pop quiz.

The Cognella Series on Student Success is a collection of books designed to help students develop the essential life and learning skills needed to support a happy, healthy, and productive higher education experience. Featuring topics suggested by students and books written by experts, the series offers research-based, yet practical advice to help any student navigate new challenges and succeed throughout their college experience.

Series Editor: Richard Parsons, Ph.D.
Professor of Counselor Education, West Chester University

Other titles available in the series:

- *A Student's Guide to Stress Management*
- *A Student's Guide to College Transition*
- *A Student's Guide to Self-Care*
- *A Student's Guide to Money Matters*
- *A Student's Guide to Communication and Self-Presentation*
- *A Student's Guide to Exercise for Improving Health*

ABOUT THE AUTHOR

I t's never too early to determine your true calling and start working toward your ideal career!

A Student's Guide to a Meaningful Career: Choices, Education, and Opportunities serves as a dynamic workbook that will help you uncover your unique qualities, passions, and strengths, then consider complementary career paths. You will learn how to take advantage of the many opportunities available to you during your academic career, many of which can make you more marketable to future employers.

Filled with thought-provoking readings, activities, and opportunities for personal reflection, this guide will help you make strategic, career-related decisions as a college student so you can realize your career aspirations in the future.

A Student's Guide to a Meaningful Career is part of the Cognella Series on Student Success, a collection of books designed to help students develop the essential life and learning skills needed to support a happy, healthy, and productive higher education experience.

Vickie Ann McCoy is a professor of counselor education at West Chester University. Prior to joining the faculty at West Chester, Dr. McCoy worked at the Institute for Disability Studies at the University of Southern Mississippi and served as the coordinator of counseling and testing services for students with disabilities at Monmouth University. She earned her doctoral degree in counseling psychology from the University of Southern Mississippi.

CONTENTS

Unit I: Your Career Calling is Personal: Who Are You?

Unit II: Your Career Dovetails With the World: Where Do You Fit?

Unit III: Actualizing Your Career: How Do You Transition From Daydream to Reality?

EDITOR'S PREFACE

The transition to college marks a significant milestone in a person's life. Many of you will be preparing to live away from your friends and family for the very first time. Clearly this is and should be an exciting time.

It is a time to experience new things and experiment with new options. While the opportunity to grow is clear—so too are the many challenges you will experience as you transition from high school to college.

Research suggests that the first year of college is the most difficult period of adjustment a student faces. Not only will you be required to adjust to new academic demands but you will also have to navigate a number of social and emotional challenges that accompany your life as a college student. The books found within this series—*Cognella Series on Student Success*—have been developed to help you with the many issues confronting your successful transition from life as a high school student to life as a collegiate. Each book within the series was designed to provide research-based, yet *practical* advice to assist you succeeding in your college experience.

One area of transition that can be very stressful is making a decision about which career path you would like to follow. Approaching the end of the high school experience is often accompanied by questions—both self and other imposed—as to what next? While there may be subtle and even not-so-subtle pressure to follow this or that path following high school, it is important that you take time for a little reflection and self-discovery. Identifying your personal interests, aptitudes, challenges, resources, and opportunities will help you identify your career calling.

The current text, *A Student's Guide to a Meaningful Career: Choices, Education, and Opportunities*, provides you with well-researched, practical advice and specific strategies to help you to identify your purpose, your passion, and your career calling. As you will soon come to discover, while the topic is serious, the manner in which the information is presented is both engaging and directly applicable to your own current life experience. The book employs case illustrations in a feature called *"Voices From Campus,"* and opportunities to apply what you are learning in a feature called *"Your Turn."* I know that you will find this, as well as the other books within the series, to be a useful guide to your successful transition from high school to college.

Richard Parsons, Ph.D.
Series Editor

AUTHOR'S PREFACE

After years of teaching a career counseling graduate course, which followed my earlier work in a career counseling and placement office on a university campus, I had a great deal to say on the subject, but no outlet other than bending the ear of unsuspecting graduate students who wandered into my office. When the series editor asked me if I wanted to write this book to help provide a bridge for young adults moving from secondary schools to their postsecondary lives of higher education, technical training, and/or work opportunities, I jumped at the chance. Who wouldn't want to break away from academic writing, with its restrictive structure, and just write in a conversational tone from personal experience? So I took a deep breath, considered my 30 plus years of experience with the topic, and wrote in the early morning hours for 10 months. Morning is such a hopeful time of day, filled with so many options, just like your career path, so it seemed a perfect time to write about possibilities.

I am most excited about the premise of this book as a workbook to explore a true career calling in your life. In a world where everyone seems to want to tell the reader what to think, believe, do, and be, I take great delight in writing a book that is, instead, an invitation for you to tell your story. This book is not a scholarly publication filled with impressive references and the wisdom of everyone who has a thought on the topic. Instead, it is a long conversation between the two of us … you just haven't written your part yet. But you will. In each chapter, I will tell you what I know about a topic, share some activities that students have found helpful over the years, and invite you to respond. The power of this book is not in my words, but in yours.

Looking back, as I began to write and write and write, I quickly came to the end of my first draft of the project with very few citations. This was different for me. It was the first time I have ever written so freely in my own voice without relying heavily on the work of others. Most of the suggestions for activities are based on processes that I have used for years in career counseling. Though they developed out of my experiences and were finely tuned by years of use, I am aware that someone before me laid the groundwork for everything I say here. However, citations become difficult for those processes we all employ in career counseling, which do not lead obviously back to a theoretical origin or author. I apologize in advance, most sincerely, for any oversights in citation that may arise from the collaborative nature of career counseling, where early mentors taught me the "tricks of the trade." I am guessing that some of my mentors and supervisors over the past 30 years should probably be acknowledged more formally, but their brilliance has blended into a single knowledge base to me, and I cannot unravel who helped me understand what. Additionally, once you work your way through this book, completing the exercises and jotting your ideas in the margins, you will become the coauthor of the completed copy you hold in your hands. Pretty cool, huh?

Vickie Ann McCoy, PhD
Author

ACKNOWLEDGMENTS

I would like to thank the series editor, Dr. Richard Parsons, and Kassie Graves and her colleagues at Cognella for giving me the opportunity to write this book. It was a rare treat to be trusted with the freedom to just write from the heart without unnecessary constraints.

I would also like to thank the wonderful volunteers who wrote the Voices From Campus essays for this book. I am amazed by their willingness to share their stories with all of you, asking nothing in return for their time and talented contributions. In their own words, these fabulous individuals are:

Kelsey Davis Onuskanych is an elementary school Counselor in Berks County, Pennsylvania. She obtained her Bachelor of Science in human development and family studies from the Pennsylvania State University and her Master of Education in K-12 School Counseling at West Chester University of Pennsylvania, where she was still a graduate student when she wrote these essays.

Rebekah prefers not to share her full name to allow her to share more freely. After graduating in 2015 with her Master's degree in Higher Education Counseling and Student Affairs, Rebekah is in the second year of her first job as a young professional. She enjoys her position which involves advocating for and supporting lesbian, gay, bisexual, transgender, queer, and questioning (LGBTQ) college students. When Rebekah is not at work she enjoys spending time with her family, writing poetry, and relaxing pastimes such as nature, arts and crafts, reading, watching TV, and cuddling with her pets.

UNIT I:
YOUR CAREER
CALLING IS PERSONAL:
WHO ARE YOU?

KNOWING YOURSELF

WHAT UNIQUE QUALITIES DO YOU POSSESS?

Until you know who you are, you cannot know what you will become.

Your future is bright and the pathways to be taken are many. As the title and saying above suggest, your career journey begins with a better understanding of yourself: What are your unique characteristics and personal values? While this personal exploration will not help you figure out where the money is or what will impress others, if you take the time to explore this chapter and get to know yourself better, you may discover your calling instead of just landing a job. Seriously, this is YOUR journey, so how can it begin anywhere other than with you? We will start your exploration with some background information from the experts, interspersed with everyday illustrations of these concepts to help you make personal meaning from what you are reading. Then, we'll provide you with some exercises for guided practice so you can document this phase of your journey. Finally, we have two volunteers who will share bits and pieces of their career path with you in this and future chapters. We hope you enjoy the journey.

1.1: What We Know

To assist you in understanding why we begin your journey here, this section begins with a brief description of the importance of self-assessment in the career planning process. In other words, what are the experts saying about why knowing yourself better is an important aspect of your career journey? To begin, some researchers studied the ways people prepare for careers and found that, if young people are motivated to engage in effective self-exploration and planning, they will be more likely to develop a calling and to clarify their career identity. These researchers went on to say that young people who are successful at this early stage will likely continue to grow personally and professionally, and increase their chances of achieving their desires and better lives (Praskova, Creed, & Hood, 2015). Wow ... that is possibly a really nice future unfolding for students who care to take the time to understand themselves early in the career process.

There are also researchers who are interested in what motivates people to begin exploring and participating in early career development tasks. Some of these experts believe that career preparatory activities (like the ones in this book) motivate people to continue on paths that lead to positive career outcomes (Phillips & Blustein, 1994). So while each small activity presented might not seem like an important part of building a career, when you put them all together, they will lead you right where you need to go ... sort of like following the yellow brick road all the way to Oz or following the yellow footprints in an Ikea store all the way to the exit.

Another way of looking at this chapter, this book, and the road ahead, is to consider the importance of understanding your own personal life story. It is difficult to isolate the career part of your life as if it is separate from you as a whole. Your career is just one part of the story of you, and it winds itself around all the other parts until it isn't just something you do, but it becomes part of who you are. From this way of looking at things, some researchers assert that young people will benefit from taking the time to explore their personal meanings, identify important life themes, and script their own narratives (personal and career stories) from their own holistic (big picture) point of view (McIlveen & Patton, 2007; Savickas, 2011). Obviously, I agree because I am writing this book for you. If you agree, I hope you will read on and begin this journey.

Self-Exploration

Understanding yourself can help you find clarity and discover how to use your career planning time and energy wisely to achieve the best result. Sounds easy enough, but it probably leaves you wondering, "Where do I begin?" Your self-exploration should probably begin with your characteristic traits, personal qualities, and preferences. If you take the time to understand your traits, qualities, and preferences, you will begin to better understand what motivates, comforts, and satisfies you; because these things affect your decision-making process both personally and professionally. So if you take the time to understand who you are, you will be equipped to begin the search for a satisfying career that fits your personal style and preferred ways of living your life.

Indeed, what you know about yourself (intrapersonal knowledge) is an important place to begin your journey of self-exploration. But don't forget that another important part of self-understanding is making sense of who you are with others (interpersonal knowledge). Experts in psychology, counseling, teaching, and related fields often use a diagram called a Johari Window (Luft & Ingham, 1961) to help us understand how we learn about ourselves from others. Basically, the idea is that there are certain things that you already know about yourself (some you choose to share and some you choose to keep private), but there are also things that other people know about you (some you know about too, but some that are unknown to you). These things that others notice about you, but which you have not yet discovered about yourself are valuable. To know yourself better, it is important to invite trusted others to share their knowledge of you, allowing you to learn more about how others experience you. Is that something you might be open to trying?

YOUR TURN 1.1

Using a Trusted Other as Your "Mirror"

Sometimes, when we are trying to assess ourselves, to understand our character, we limit our self-understanding because it is difficult to look in a mirror and see ourselves objectively. Perhaps we are too critical, or perhaps too kind, or maybe we focus on just one trait and miss other interesting things about ourselves. When this is the situation, sometimes it helps to use a trusted friend or family member as a "mirror." To hear someone else express observations about you can be an enlightening look in a different mirror. Care to give it a try?

Ask someone you trust to tell you some things about yourself. Ask this person to go deeper than surface observations. Ask "Can you tell me something about me that shows you really 'get me' and understand things about me that maybe not everyone sees right away?"

Did the response help you feel totally understood? (If not, perhaps you can ask another person the same thing and see if the response is different.)

- What did this person see in you? What did this person "get" about you? Is this an important component of your identity?
- What have you learned about yourself through the eyes of another?
- Put this new knowledge together with what you already understand about yourself to form a bigger perspective.

Values in Action

Let's begin by defining values. Values are what you really care about. Right now, your values may pertain more to your personal life, but they will also impact your satisfaction with your career and your day-to-day enjoyment of your work life. Identifying and understanding your values can help you to determine both your personal and career goals. This clarity can lead to making better decisions about your career and your personal life as you will understand how the two dovetail to create a meaningful work–life balance which reflects your unique values. When you understand your values, you are also in a better position to select the types of careers and work environments that best match your own needs and preferences.

Many experts also believe that a better understanding of yourself and your values will help you understand why you are drawn to certain types of people and how others with similar values may be drawn to the same fields as you. You will also be better able to understand any differences or conflicts that you may experience based on value differences between you and your future colleagues (Hofstede, 1984).

In an attempt to better understand how your values in action, also known as character strengths, can become a tool for you to use in understanding yourself better on this career exploration journey, perhaps you would like to take the VIA Inventory of Strengths (VIA-IS) (Peterson & Seligman, 2004). Using this tool, you will be able to identify your positive strengths, and best of all it is free. To access this 15-minute version, go to www.viacharacter.org and be sure to pick the VIA Youth Survey version if you are between the ages of 10 and 17 or the VIA Adult Survey if you are 18 or older.

YOUR TURN 1.2

Values in Action/Character Strengths

Directions: After completing your 15-minute online VIA Survey (youth or adult) at www.viacharacter.org and receiving your ordered list of 24 character strengths* that represent your values in action, respond to the following:

- Looking at your top three to five strengths, do these seem like words you would use to describe yourself? (If not, do you see descriptors further down your list which seem to describe you better?)

- Has anyone else ever used these words to describe you? (If not, do you see descriptors further down your list that others have used to describe you?)

- Can you share a story about a time you remember saying or doing something that demonstrated one of these characteristics in action? (If not, look further down your list until you see one that resonates with a specific memory.)

- Are there values in action or characteristics not on this list that you would like to add to your collection of personally descriptive words? What do these additional words mean to you? How do you demonstrate them in your day-to-day life?

*If you chose not to take the actual VIA Survey, you can use your intuition to just circle the words here that "feel right" to you:

Wisdom and Knowledge Strengths

- Creativity
- Curiosity
- Judgment
- Love of Learning
- Perspective

Courage Strengths

- Bravery
- Perseverance
- Honesty
- Zest

Humanity Strengths

- Love
- Kindness
- Social Intelligence

Justice Strengths

- Teamwork
- Fairness
- Leadership

Temperance Strengths

- Forgiveness
- Humility
- Prudence
- Self-Regulation

Transcendence Strengths

- Appreciation of Beauty and Excellence
- Gratitude
- Hope
- Humor
- Spirituality

Personal Characteristics

So the VIA-IS you just completed gave you some information about enduring character strengths we call traits. As you begin to learn more about your individual traits, you will understand yourself better and begin to see some of the unique ways you can contribute to a career field. Most experts believe that these traits are relatively permanent and do not change much over the course of your life or from one setting (school?) to another (work?). Do you recognize those aspects of yourself that seem to be fairly stable? Have your family members told stories about things you did as a child that leave you thinking, "Yup, that sounds like me. I'm still like that." Those aspects of yourself that remain constant are your traits, or as some folks would say, they begin to define who you are.

But what about those changing moods and aspects of yourself that seem to be different when you are home or with friends; well rested or tired; content or hangry? We call these changing patterns states. A state is a temporary or changing pattern of characteristics that appear under certain circumstances or as reactions to some outside influences. We may find ourselves in states where we feel confident, fearful, competent, shy, or anxious. When we use the word "states," we are typically using it to describe a person's reaction to something. The key to understanding the difference is to think about how you typically are (traits) and how you temporarily change (state) in certain settings or under certain circumstances. So what might you need to know about your states and how they can influence your career path?

Some experts believe that our states, our moods and emotions, affect all aspects of our lives including attitudes toward work and our workplace situations. For example, when you dislike one of your courses, do you feel unhappy in that class? Do you also notice yourself developing a bad attitude toward that class? When that happens do you ever procrastinate, drag out the assignments, and/or rush to finish without putting your best efforts toward it? If this is something you have experienced, but is not the way you normally approach things, then you now understand how a state can lead to attitudes and behaviors that are not reflective of your usual traits. The same thing can happen as you choose a career path—your state can impact your attitude and affect how much effort you are willing to put into that career, or right now, how much effort you are willing to put into this workbook and your early career path exploration. If you are feeling confident, hopeful, and excited about the journey ahead, you are more likely to stay with this exploration, but if you are feeling doubtful, discouraged, or bored, you are probably more likely to toss this book aside for now. See how even now, your state can impact your career? Your transient moods and emotions can influence your behavior: negative attitudes and emotions can negatively impact your career journey, while positive attitudes and emotions can lead to career satisfaction (Bauer & Erdogan, 2010).

YOUR TURN 1.3

Chart Your States

Directions: Fill in this chart a few times each day, from home, school, work, activities and while alone, with family, and with friends. Notice how your mood states change under differing circumstances. What might this mean about your potential attitude toward differing types of work settings? Can you imagine how this chart might have looked different when you were younger? How it might be different several years from now?

What time is it?	Where am I?	Who am I with?	Am I tired?	Am I hungry?	What emotions am I feeling?	Is this emotional state consistent with my usual traits?

Moods and feelings change in different circumstances and over time. It is important to remember that different career options may be more appealing at different phases of your life because of your fluctuating states, moods, and attitudes. For this reason, we lean more heavily on information pertaining to enduring traits when selecting careers, but we can still use our fluctuating states to understand workplace rhythms that would positively influence our job satisfaction along the way.

1.2: How Others Use This Information

Understanding your values, characteristics, traits, and states and being able to articulate these things to others will be helpful along the journey. Your high school counselor can use this information to assist you in selecting a college, technical school, apprenticeship, or other postsecondary option that is a good fit for you as a unique individual. Your college advisor or employment counselor can use this same information to help you select a major course of study and/or a field of work which is compatible with who you are. As you enter the world of work, either directly or as an intern or apprentice, your supervisor can use knowledge of your strengths and values to guide you in working effectively with colleagues.

Many successful individuals have been where you are now ... standing at the very beginning of the adult career path. They have used this information in very different ways to guide the numerous large and small choices that define a career path. Two of these individuals have agreed to share their journeys with you throughout this book.

Kelsey's Corner (A Graduate Student's Perspective)
Who Am I?

To me, whenever a teacher in high school asked me what my values were, I had no idea what that really meant. Yes, family was important and yes, I was an honest person, but what did that really mean? Who was I? This was a question I often filled with the basics: honest, kind, respectful of others, and so on. It wasn't until I got to college that I had to really think about what was important to me. I guess you could consider me a late value bloomer. My values really started to form in college just during daily interactions with other students. I would simply be eating dinner with other girls on my floor and find myself thinking, "I could never do that" or "Don't you feel bad?" And don't get me wrong, these thoughts were rarely judgmental, rather, reflective of what I would do in those situations. Once those thoughts were rolling, I began to view my classes differently. You know that voice in the back of your head that speaks up in high school and constantly asks, "When will I ever need this again?" Well, that's the thought I had in some of my classes. I would think about whether studying this particular subject for four years would fit who I am as a person. There it was again. Who is Kelsey? When I took my first college psychology class, I knew immediately I wanted to work with people. Human development, how the brain works, and why people behave the way they do were just fascinating to me. There's value number one: I want to interact with people every day and really get to know them. The longer I thought about it, I had always been that friend in the group that the rest of the friends came to as the advice-giver or problem solver. Then I started taking counseling classes. For me, this was the best thing to happen because I really felt like those were MY people. They just understood me. Then the values started rolling in: I want to help people; I believe that all people should be accepted no matter what; I believe that people have bad days and should not be judged on that; I believe family has an important part in who you are as a person; and the list went on. Finally, I understood what a value was. A value is something you live by and may not know it's a value until you have to think about it. A value is something that makes you say, "Yeah, I agree," or "Wait a minute, why?" A value is what makes you who you are as a person. Now, of course it's more complex than this, but that is how I came to understand it myself. Values just make sense to you, because they are you. Now, here comes that question again. Who are YOU?

VOICES FROM CAMPUS 1.2

Rebekah's Voice (A New Professional's Perspective)

When I was eight years old, I decided I was going to be a teacher when I grew up. I told everyone and was determined to accomplish this goal. In doing so, I diligently studied different aspects of my teachers in elementary school and middle school, paying attention and thinking "I like the way they teach x subject" or "I'd teach y subject in a more creative way." I never once thought I'd veer away from this path. In high school, I had to take a career exploration class in which I was assigned to shadow someone in the career I was most interested in pursuing. So I chose to shadow a teacher at the elementary school I attended. I had to write some reflection and still was convinced this was the right path for me. Also, during high school, I started to really establish that my favorite subject was English. I wrote for the school newspaper, took college prep

English classes, and even took a creative writing class. So when it was time to apply for college, I chose secondary English education as my major. I was going to go to college to become a high school English teacher!

Now, here is where my career path shifts. After my first semester in college, I realized I was not the best at writing and had a horrible time with grammar (I still do even as a young professional). I didn't enjoy reading what professors told me to read and some of my classes were boring to me. So for my second semester, I switched to history secondary education, which also ended up boring me. But I stuck with it, because since I was eight years old I had been telling people that I would be a teacher!

One thing I did right my first year in college was to join the LGBTQA club. As an out lesbian, I knew equality and acceptance were important to me (a value which I hold to this day). Through this, I met some students who majored in women's & gender studies. So I decided I'd take an introduction to women's studies class over the summer, thinking that if I hated it I only had to suffer through five weeks. Well, this class literally changed my life and I was sad it ended so quickly. As soon as the fall semester started, I completed my change of major form from education to women's & gender studies and that began my new journey to where I am today.

As I reflect on my undergraduate career, one thing I'm thankful for is the encouragement I got from others to try something new (the summer class). Had I not listened to them I may have gone on taking classes I didn't enjoy and hating every minute of it. Did I feel like I let some people down since I decided I no longer wanted to be a teacher? Yes, I did feel that way and I'm sure I did disappoint some people, but I knew it was my life, my career, and I had to do what was right for me. You know when you feel something in your "gut"—it's usually right. So be open to listening to others, but ultimately find what's right for you.

1.3: How You Can Use This Information

And just like that, you have completed this first chapter and your journey is underway. Congratulations! I hope you found the exploration meaningful. Though many people choose to begin the journey with explorations of interests and aptitudes, I think you made a good choice to assess your characteristics here in Chapter 1 first. You can use this new knowledge in many facets of your life, but of course, we introduced it here as an essential first step on your career journey. Armed with this growing understanding of your unique characteristics, you are encouraged to move on to Chapter 2 where you will begin to explore where your interests lie.

1.4: Want More?

Don't forget that you have more opportunities to explore in the "Where to Turn" appendices at the end of this book, where you will find resources *In Print, On the Web,* and *On Campus.*

1.5: The Take Away

- Your career is just one part of the story of you, and it winds itself around all the other parts until it isn't just something you do, but it becomes part of who you are.

- Understanding your values, characteristics, traits, and states and being able to articulate these things to others will be helpful along the journey.

References

Bauer, T., & Erdogan, B. (2010). *Organizational behavior.* Irvington, NY: Flat World Knowledge Inc.

Hofstede, G. (1984). *Culture's consequences: International differences in work-related values* (Vol. 5). Thousand Oaks: SAGE Publications.

Luft, J., & Ingham, H. (1961). The Johari Window: A graphic model of awareness in interpersonal relations. *Human Relations Training News, 5*(9), 6-7.

McIlveen, P. F., & Patton, W. A. (2007). Narrative career counselling: Theory and exemplars of practice. *Australian Psychologist, 42*(3), 226-235. doi: 10.1080/00050060701405592

Peterson, C., & Seligman, M. (2004). *Character Strengths and Virtues: A Handbook and Classification.* Washington, DC: APA Press.

Phillips, S. D., & Blustein, D. L. (1994). Readiness for career choices: Planning, exploring, and deciding. *The Career Development Quarterly, 43*(1), 63-73.

Praskova, A., Creed, P., & Hood, M. (2015). Career identity and the complex mediating relationships between career preparatory actions and career progress markers. *Journal of Vocational Behavior, 87,* 145-153. http://dx.doi.org/10.1016/j.jvb.2015.01.001

Savickas, M. L. (2011). Constructing careers: Actor, agent, and author. *Journal of Employment Counseling, 48*(4), 179-182.

EXPLORING YOUR INTERESTS

WHAT DRAWS YOUR ATTENTION?

Know what you like, like what you do and you will be more likely to be motivated for career success.

First, I want to say that it is perfectly okay if you do not yet know what you want to do when you are finished with school. In fact, let's not even try to answer that question yet—we'll save it for a later chapter. (Whew ... what a relief, right?) For right now, let's just spend some time figuring what you like. Try not to overthink it just yet. If I ask you what draws your attention, what is your gut response? Please listen to yourself ... you are the expert on you and you already know what you like. These preferences become our interests, and the experts in career development pretty much agree that we need to pay close attention to our innate interests if we want to find our calling instead of just a job. Ready? Let's explore.

2.1: What We Know

Career counseling experts who specialize in helping young people assess their interests generally agree that interest inventories are a helpful starting point in the process (Timmons, Podmostko, Bremer, Lavin, & Wills, 2005). Career interest inventories typically describe or illustrate many work-related tasks and ask you to rate how much you would enjoy doing each task. When these inventories are scored, they can help you recognize your interests and preferences. For example, an inventory may ask you to check whether you prefer building a birdhouse or reading a book about birds. If you've always known you have fondness for birds, a question like this will help you begin to hone your understanding of where your preference for birds intersects with other preferences you hold to yield your unique work interests. That knowledge is added to other preferences such as whether you prefer to complete a project independently or as part of a team. There are no right or wrong answers to any of these questions, but how you respond helps clarify your preferences for activities you enjoy and types of work you might prefer. These preferences are called interests.

When we look at the history of interest inventories, we learn that nearly 100 years ago, psychologists noticed that people working in the same areas often shared similar interests. Even more interesting was the fact that sometimes these interests had little to do with the job itself, yet folks who enjoyed that type of work tended to have these preferences and interests in common. They realized that a person's interests could possibly be used to determine which fields of work a person might enjoy. One of the most well-known psychologists who studied this connection was Edward K. Strong, who developed the first interest inventory in 1927. That instrument has been revised many, many times over the years and its name changed often as well. We now call it the Strong Interest Inventory (SII) and it remains one of the most popular self-assessment tools in use today, along with similar instruments such as the Kuder Occupational Interest Survey, the Self-Directed Search, and the Campbell Interest and Skill Survey (Harrington & Long, 2013). These are all instruments which your counselor can administer if you have an interest.

2.2: Ready to Clarify Your Interests?

Sometimes, in the search for quick answers, folks skip straight to aptitude/ability tests and then they end up working in areas where they are really good, but they hate their jobs anyway. Think about it. Are you good at something that you don't really enjoy? Would you want to do this every day for many years? This happens for some people, but we don't want it to happen to you, so let's take some steps to help you clarify your interests. Interests are essential to career success because interests are what motivates us to want to do particular things. It just makes sense, doesn't it? You are more likely to be more satisfied with your career if it permits you to do things you like, so it's a really good idea to clarify your interests now. Then, later on, you can choose a career that matches well with these interests. See the cycle? Know what you like, like what you do, and you will be more likely to be motivated for career success.

So to begin your informal interest exploration, let's think about how you like to spend you free time lately? When you have a few hours to yourself, do you like to walk a dog? Practice your sport? Read a great book? Organize your clothes? Write poetry? Sing along with your playlist?

Tinker with electronics? Volunteer for a good cause? Meet up with your friends? Strum a few chords? Scroll through social media sites? Or, perhaps … another way to think about your interests is to move away from just thinking about these activities you currently enjoy and to spend some time reflecting more generally on what has always drawn your attention (remember our state/trait discussion in Chapter 1?). Some of the things you enjoy now give you meaningful information about your interests, but they may be temporary (like states) and influenced by your environments, your friends, and your stage of life. Because of this, you might want to also think about your enduring interests (like traits) which have been stable over the years. What has routinely drawn your attention over the years? For example: Have you always been drawn to animals? Has music always been your go-to balm on a difficult day? Do you feel more alive when you are exercising? Have you always taken things apart to see how they work? Have you always been fascinated by the news, popular culture, current events, or the arts? If you don't really remember, perhaps you can ask people who have known you most of your life if they have seen a pattern in your attention and interest.

YOUR TURN 2.1

Chart Your Preferences

Directions: List a few options under each prompt. Can you remember (perhaps with help from others) how this chart might have looked different when you were younger? How it might be different several years from now? Which of these environmental preferences would you consider to be enduring preferences?

When you look around, what draws your stare?	When you have a choice, what sounds do you prefer?	Do you like sitting or standing or moving?	Do you prefer texts or voice or Facetime/ Skype, or in-person conversation? Or no conversation?	More alone time? Or working side by side? Or collabo- rating with others?	People, animals, objects, or ideas ... what draws your atten- tion?	Money, food, art, clothes, technolo- gy, Netflix, social media, your cat, and/or ...? What rocks your world?

2.3: What Inventories Can You Try?

So you have now tried thinking about your interests on your own, but there are just so many things to consider at once and it can all begin to jumble together. Perhaps it would be easier to organize your thoughts if you used a system of guided questions to help lead you to your preferences and interests, especially as they pertain to the world of work. If you are ready to try an interest inventory or two, you have several options available to you. Your school counselors and/or your college career counselors would be happy to administer and interpret an interest inventory with you. They might offer you paper inventories, if scan-trons are your thing, or they can offer you access to online guidance systems such as CHOICES, SIGI+, DISCOVER, or O*NET. But if you are ready to begin on your own now, you can access the free U.S. Department of Labor O*NET Interest Profiler at https://www.mynextmove.org/explore/ip. This is a very popular interest inventory, but it asks about experiences that many people your age have not yet had. So perhaps you'd prefer to begin with a more simple interest activity geared for younger adults like yourself.

YOUR TURN 2.2

Brainstorm Your Interests

Here is a quick and easy way to explore some work-related interests which might become clues to areas you can consider exploring further. Circle any of the following areas that you would consider interests, and feel free to brainstorm a bit and write in more of your own. When you are finished, perhaps you can speak with someone you trust and explain what you like about the interests you circled.

Drawing	Gardening/Horticulture	Tennis
Animals	Construction	Research
Teaching	Travel	Camping
Photography	Reading	Counseling
Nutrition	Drug Abuse/Alcoholism Treatment	Rehabilitation
Foreign Languages	Consumer Advocacy	Video Games
Climbing	City Planning	Animals
Automobiles	Mathematics	Planning Events
Books	Machines	Cooking
Watching Television	Criminal Justice/Corrections	Healthcare
Writing	Design	Politics
Solar Energy	Music Videos	Dancing
Green Energy	Editing Videos	Architecture
Flying	Yoga	Computers
Environmental Issues	Rock Climbing	Law
International Affairs	Sports	Insects
Internet Research	Social Networking Sites	Backpacking
Landscaping	Scuba Diving	Mechanical Things

Electronics	Aerospace	Politics
Armed Forces	Financial Matters	Biotechnology
Broadcasting	Energy	Entrepreneurship
Filmmaking	Foreign Service	Franchising
Government	Art/Creativity	Real Estate
Meditation	Robotics	Sales
Health/Nutrition	Theatre	Pottery
Software	Rocks	Weather
Spirituality	Management	Aquaculture
Astronomy	Public Relations	Ethnic Studies
Reading	Clothes/Fashion	Disability
Investigation	Cycling	Horses
————	————	————
————	————	————
————	————	————
————	————	————

Whether you prefer to work with a professional counselor at this time or tinker around the free online assessments on your own for a while, there are some common guidelines for taking these types of inventories. Generally speaking, you will be given a series of items and forced to choose between two pairs or to use a like/dislike scale to rate an activity. As you work through the items, it is generally best to work fairly quickly (trying not to overthink each item) and to respond as honestly as possible. When completing interest inventories, you might also want to remember that there are no right or wrong answers, and you are expected to focus only on preferences and interests, NOT on skills or training (those factors come into play in later chapters).

2.4: How Others Use This Information

As in the previous chapter, two people have generously agreed to share their exploration of interests with you, because they both hope that reading about their journeys will help you as you take this next step.

Kelsey's Corner (A Graduate Student's Perspective)

"What do you want to do?" is a loaded question in any situation, but it never seems to provoke more anxious or defensive feelings than when it is asked in the context of careers. For some, the answer is very simple and immediate. For others, this conversation is plagued with hesitation and avoidance. You may be hearing societal expectations in the back of your head including how much money you should make and what benefits you should get. You may also be feeling pressure from family members who expect you to achieve certain career goals. I was one of the lucky few who heard both! Every time I was excited to talk to my roommate or my sister about a class I really enjoyed, I was always hit with, "That's great, but you'll never find a job." These seemingly harmless sentiments actually do more damage than people expect. I would find myself thinking that they were right and maybe I wasn't interested in that topic. While money, family opinions, and benefits are all important to consider, that is not something that needs to be decided at this moment. Right now it is important to focus on your interests because let's face it, life would be utterly boring and tedious without them. Just as with anything else in life, identifying your interests is a process. For me, I have always been fascinated with human development/behavior as well as nutrition and astronomy. How did I know I was interested in these topics? Well, I would watch documentaries or TV shows about them in my free time. Another clear indicator for me was that out of all the classes I took, both in high school and college, these were the classes that the coursework didn't feel like work. So what is that to you? Think of a topic, or multiple topics, that you genuinely enjoy. Don't let this stress you out. Let all of the thoughts about salaries and societal expectations drift away until Chapter 7. Identifying an interest right now doesn't necessarily mean that it will be your career down the line. At this point in the process, listening to yourself is the key to finding your fit. No, you may not know what career you are going to choose just yet, but look on the bright side! Now when someone asks you "What do you want to do" you can answer with, "Well, I'm not sure, but I know I like [insert YOUR interests here]."

VOICES FROM CAMPUS 2.2

Rebekah's Voice (A New Professional's Perspective)

Remember in my first story how I tried something new and discovered I really liked it? Well I did it a second time and took an intro to sociology class. Learning about human behavior and about people's cultures was fascinating to me. So I added sociology as a major as well. These were topics I was interested in learning. When I told people I changed my major, the first question I was asked was "What are you going to do with that?" and it made me question my decision to no longer major in education. But as I mentioned earlier, I knew in my gut this was what I wanted to study.

I'm not going to lie, this question made me very nervous. I wondered if I had made the wrong choice, but I turned to my academic advisor and expressed my concerns. She told me the beauty of my majors was that they are flexible and I'm not pigeonholed to only one option. She told me it may seem cliché, but when people ask me that question, even though I may not know what I want to do, I can answer with "Anything I want to do." And she was right. The majors I chose were flexible. I looked into what other graduates went on to do as careers after they graduated. Learning about what others went on to do didn't mean that I had made a final decision about what

I wanted to do, but it helped me have confidence in the answer of "Anything I want."

I knew my interest in the subjects I was learning would give me a head start in figuring out what I wanted to do after graduation. I enjoyed what I was learning. I was given the ability to research topics I found intriguing, complete independent studies, and present at conferences on the research I had done. I say all of this to emphasize that you need to do what is right for YOU. The voices in the back of your head, or in front of your face, may never go away. To this day, my brother still thinks I majored in "fluff," but I am okay with his opinion because I did what was right for me. I am happy in my career, and that is what is most important.

2.5: How You Can Use This Information

Now that you have completed this second chapter and, hopefully, gained a better understanding of your interests, you are really getting underway on this self-exploration. Congratulations! I genuinely hope you are finding this journey meaningful. Now that you know what draws your attention and holds your interest, you are encouraged to move on to Chapter 3 where you will begin to explore your aptitudes, or the things you do quite well.

2.6: Want More?

Don't forget that you have more opportunities to explore in the "Where to Turn" appendices at the end of this book, where you will find resources *In Print, On the Web,* and *On Campus.*

2.7: The Take Away

- • You are more likely to be satisfied with your career if it permits you to do things you like, so it's a really good idea to clarify your interests now.

- • Career counseling experts who specialize in helping young people assess their interests generally agree that interest inventories are a helpful starting point in the process.

References

Harrington, T., & Long, J. (2013). The history of interest inventories and career assessments in career counseling. *The Career Development Quarterly, 61*, 83–92. doi:10.1002/j.2161-0045.2013.00039.x

Timmons, J., Podmostko, M., Bremer, C., Lavin, D., & Wills, J. (2005). Career planning begins with assessment: A guide for professionals serving youth with educational and career development challenges (revised edition). Washington, DC: National Collaborative on Workforce and Disability for Youth, Institute for Educational Leadership.

EVALUATING YOUR APTITUDES AND ABILITIES

WHAT DO YOU DO WELL?

Education is not the piling on of learning, information, data, facts, skills, or abilities—that's training or instruction—but is rather making visible what is hidden as a seed.

— Thomas Moore

So let's start with an old debate—what is the difference between an aptitude and an ability (or skill)? You'll find these words used interchangeably at times, but they do have different meanings. Essentially, the word aptitude generally refers to an innate competence or talent—something that we are born with (remember our discussion of traits?), while ability (or skill) is more transient over time and can be developed as needed or wanted (like the states we discussed). Though there is a distinction between the two, for this chapter we will be talking about both, at times lumped together, as we move our discussion from the things you want to do into the realm of the things you can do.

3.1: What We Know

As we begin to investigate aptitudes, the literature becomes argumentative, primarily because many so-called aptitude tests actually measure existing abilities and skills. In other words, measuring potential is a tricky game. So when we decide to start figuring out what we can do well or might do well given a certain set of circumstances, it can all become confusing and over-whelming. To keep it relatively simple and user friendly, let's just examine ways to learn a bit more about your unique abilities, those you have already begun developing as skills and those that still hover in the background as raw potential.

When we begin to consider all of the ability- and skills-based instru-ments, we quickly learn that many measure a combination of interests and skills, which will be helpful for you if you decide to try one with your school counselor or career counselor. But if you are looking for instruments which give you feedback about specific abilities and skills, you will quickly find that many question-and-answer type inventories cannot give you the information you seek. How can you answer a set of questions that will tell you if you sing well, bake delicious cookies, or have an eye for combining color and texture? The problem is that many inventory scores are not relevant for abilities that fall outside of traditional skills, so things like sales initiative, lead-ership potential, management skills, organizational aptitude, creative ability, artistic talents, and competent social interaction skills are too often ignored because they can't be easily assessed by standard question-and-answer, pencil-and-paper, or computerized inventories. Though there are some very specific skills inventories for specific fields, a person would need to be seriously considering one of those fields to go down that road. So if you are still considering all possibilities and looking to get a more general sense of where your strengths lie, you will most likely be drawn to the self-assessment tests offered by your counselor. But in order for these to be fairly accurate, your self-assessment has to be accurate, which can be difficult if your experiences have been limited. In other words, how can you assess whether you would be competent at operating heavy equipment if you aren't able to drive a car yet? Or how would you know if you are good with children if you are the youngest person in your family and have never worked with kids? Your inventory scores are sometimes only as meaningful as your ability to guess at your aptitudes and abilities. We need to look at ways to help you understand yourself better, so that your self-estimate is more accurate ... and this usually comes from experience. Experiences with all sorts of activities and conversations with others about where your strengths lie will give you the valuable information you need about yourself to successfully complete ability-/skills-based inventories.

3.2: How Can You Assess Your Skills?

As you begin to consider specific careers, you will be able to find all sorts of checklists and other assessment tools online which will help you begin to evaluate your potential for success in a given career. But for these specific tools to be helpful, you need to have a few specific fields in mind. So what if you are still early in the game and considering all options? What types of things can you do to start taking stock of what you bring to the table? Well, there is a really old-school activity that has worked for years to help folks start to identify their skills and abilities. Are you willing to try something that does not involve technology or scan-tron sheets? The goal of this activity is to create a list of current skills so you know what you have to work with, what might be missing, and what you want to improve. If you are willing, you need a stack of index cards (or small sheets of paper) and a pen …

YOUR TURN 3.1

An Old-School Card Sorting Activity

Sometimes, when people ask us what our skills are or what we are good at, we just freeze. We say things like, "Uhmmm … well … I don't really know what my skills are and I'm not sure I'm really good at anything." We both know this isn't true, but sometimes, if we haven't really thought about it before, we get "stuck" because the question is huge and we sometimes don't even recognize our unique abilities and skills as important: we think they are just things we do but we disconnect them from conversations about fields of study and careers. So … ready to "unstick" yourself? Got those cards (or papers) and pen handy? Try this:

1. Jot down your ideas: What can you do? What are you good at? What comes naturally for you? This activity is all about quantity, not quality. Don't fuss about the phrasing or your handwriting or worry about duplication or detail … just list one skill per card (paper) and keep going, using as many cards (papers) as you can. Please don't be humble. If you can do it, list it. Just because something is easy for you or considered a silly hobby doesn't mean it isn't a skill.

2. Now look for patterns: Now that you've made your skills cards, flip back through them and you'll probably start to notice something interesting. Are some of these cards related? Can you sort them into groups? You can group them however you like … whatever works best for you! Deal them into piles that make sense to you. Perhaps something like "Skills

that make me happy when I'm using them," "Skills that others might pay me to use," "Skills that could use some fine-tuning," and "Skills I don't use much, but could." Or use any sorting pattern that makes sense to you. The point is to go from brainstorming skills to beginning to make sense of all your abilities.

3. If you want to give this activity some time to grow, perhaps you can carry some extra cards with you and continue to collect skills cards as you live your daily life and remember other things you do. Jot them down on the go and add them to your sorting process each evening. (Note to tech savvy millennials: Yes, of course you can just type them into an app on your phone, but if you can trust this old timer, I believe there is something worthwhile about handwriting and manually sorting and re-sorting your actual cards for clarity.)

4. If you are still stuck, perhaps you can consider giving a stack of blank cards to a friend or family member and ask them to write down what they think your skills are. They might surprise you.

3.3: What Inventories Can Help You?

In addition to the formal assessments which your counselor can administer and interpret for you, such as The Self-Directed Search (SDS) and the Campbell Interest and Skill Survey (CISS), the U.S. Department of Labor sponsors the free Career One Stop page, which offers a Skills Profiler: https://www.careerinfonet.org/skills/default.aspx?nodeid=20. You can use this page in two different ways, either by entering a career of interest and evaluating your skills for that field or by evaluating your skills first and exploring careers that fit your skills.

Recently, in addition to understanding skills and abilities which dovetail with specific professions, employers and career counselors have begun placing greater emphasis on a collection of skills known as "soft skills." Soft skills are those which pertain to character development, socio-emotional competence, and other desirable skills (such as people skills and self-management skills) which are valued across disciplines and fields. The philosophy is that once you choose a career pathway, your courses, mentors, and supervisors will help you cultivate the specific hard skills you need for that field, but they may assume that you already possess self-management soft skills. Want to see if you already have some soft skills in your skill set?

YOUR TURN 3.2

Soft Skills Assessment

Here is a list of self-management skills which employers and co-workers would probably appreciate.

To the left of each skill, please check all those which you believe you have developed. Feel free to put a question mark if it is a skill you are working on but need more time to develop.

To the right of each skill, ask a trusted friend or family member to check off skills they have seen you exhibit.

How does your perception line up with theirs? What can you do about any gap in perspectives?

_____ Adaptable _____	_____ Diplomatic _____
_____ Adventuresome _____	_____ Effective _____
_____ Articulate _____	_____ Efficient _____
_____ Assertive _____	_____ Emotionally Stable _____
_____ Ambitious _____	_____ Enthusiastic _____
_____ Candid _____	_____ Follows Instructions _____
_____ Competent _____	_____ Friendly _____
_____ Confident _____	_____ Flexible _____
_____ Courteous _____	_____ Hard-Working _____
_____ Cooperative _____	_____ Honest _____
_____ Decisive _____	_____ Knowledgeable _____
_____ Dependable _____	_____ Loyal _____

_____ Mature _____		_____ Reliable _____	
_____ Motivated _____		_____ Resourceful _____	
_____ Optimistic _____		_____ Self-Starter _____	
_____ Orderly _____		_____ Sense of Humor _____	
_____ Outgoing _____		_____ Sensitive to Others _____	
_____ Patient _____		_____ Sincere _____	
_____ Persistent _____		_____ Tactful _____	
_____ Punctual _____		_____ Talented _____	
_____ Quiet _____		_____ Trustworthy _____	
_____ Performs Under Pressure _____			

3.4: How Others Use This Information

As in the previous chapters, our wonderful volunteers have written essays documenting their journey to understand their skills and aptitudes. They hope their decision to share is helpful to you at this stage of your exploration.

VOICES FROM CAMPUS 3.1

Kelsey's Corner (A Graduate Student's Perspective)

If you're like me, talking about how great you are to other people can be a little uncomfortable, almost like you are bragging. I can't tell you how many times someone has asked me, "What do you like the most about yourself?" and I answered with, "Well I guess I like my smile." In reality I was thinking, "I'm so good at writing and grammar, I could probably write a book." Maybe we are just extremely humble, or maybe we really don't see ourselves as being experts at things. Whatever it is, without talking about what you're good at, it's going to be hard to pick a "path." So not only is it hard enough to talk about all the things we're good at, but now we have to try and decide if it is just an interest or an actual skill? I'll be honest; in high school

I was very full of myself, just not openly to people. I was a straight A student, taking all honors and advanced placement classes and there wasn't anything I could do wrong, academically at least. Well, then college came along and slapped that down pretty fast. During my first semester I took an astronomy class because the stars and planets are pretty cool. Little did I know that I actually had to understand physics in that class because, well, gravity. After that semester, I decided that math and science were not in my "skills" category. So now what? That experience moved nutrition, astronomy, and geology from my "things I really enjoy and want to pursue" list to my "things I still really enjoy but maybe I'll just read other people's research on it" list. It was back to the drawing board so to speak. That's when I was encouraged to look a little deeper into my skill sets and find those reoccurring themes that must mean something. And there was my answer—not only do I love working with people, but I am good at it! My skills included public speaking, collaborating with others to solve problems, openness, and ability to clearly communicate. Yes, I was extremely uncomfortable the whole time my career counselor asked me to verbally list at least 10 things I was good at, but in the end, if I didn't push myself to just "brag" a little bit, I may still be searching for that answer.

VOICES FROM CAMPUS 3.2

Rebekah's Voice (A New Professional's Perspective)

Throughout my entire life I've been a self-doubter: Partially because I have an older brother who is very smart and never had to study to earn As in school and partially because I have a visual disability that prevents me from doing certain things (like driving) or doing certain things as quickly as others (like reading a regular print book). I had to work twice as hard to accomplish the same thing my brother did (earn good grades) and sometimes didn't get the same results. I say this to show that one example of my skill set is persistence. This is a skill I didn't recognize I had because it was just something I did and had to do to be successful.

Sometimes our skills are so subtle it's hard to recognize them. That is one reason I think talking to family or close friends is a great way to explore what skills you may already possess but don't see in yourself. One phrase my friends have always said to me is, "thanks for listening" after they tell me a story about a hardship they went through. This helped me realize I'm good at giving others the opportunity to express their feelings.

Although I decided being a teacher wasn't the right career path for me, I engaged in other activities that gave me the opportunity to share the experience of learning (which I do enjoy) without making it my job. I became the new member educator for my fraternity and an orientation leader in college. Being able to teach new members of my organization about the fraternity and (for incoming first-year students) about the institution came naturally to me and I enjoyed doing it.

After you complete the activities offered to you, one other thing I highly suggest you do is figure out what skills you have that you also enjoy doing. My career path did not lead me to be a teacher per se, but there are aspects of my job that allow me to use this skill, such as training staff or student workers on diversity and inclusivity (remember I value equality?). It may seem overwhelming at first and you may get stuck, but knowing your skills will help you figure out which road you want to travel on towards your future career. Take some time to think about it. You don't need to have all the answers today.

3.5: How You Can Use This Information

Now that you have completed this third chapter and, hopefully, gained a better understanding of the unique skills and assets you bring to the world of work, you have the three key pieces to your puzzle. Congratulations! But before we look at that puzzle as a whole, let's put in that last key piece (because no one enjoys a jigsaw with a piece missing!). Let's move beyond the traditional three-pronged approach (Values/Interests/Abilities) and add something that makes your career journey move beyond the status of "good choice" and into the realm of finding your calling. Let's move on to Chapter 4 where you can explore your passions and determine where your energy flows.

3.6: Want More?

Don't forget that you have more opportunities to explore in the "Where to Turn" appendices at the end of this book, where you will find resources *In Print, On the Web,* and *On Campus.*

3.7: The Take Away

- •The focus of this chapter is to examine ways to learn a bit more about your unique abilities, those you have already begun developing as skills and those that still hover in the background as raw potential.

- There is a difference between aptitude (potential) and ability (skills), and it will take a careful exploration of both to understand what you bring to the table as you plan a career path.

Reference

Moore, T. (1996). *The education of the heart.* Australia: Hachette.

CHAPTER

4

DEFINING YOUR PASSIONS

WHERE DOES YOUR ENERGY FLOW?

I believe there's a calling for all of us. I know that every human being has value and purpose. The real work of our lives is to become aware. And awakened. To answer the call.

— Oprah Winfrey

In this chapter, we want to move beyond the traditional three-pronged approach (Values/Interests/Abilities) we covered in Chapters 1 through 3. We want to add a fourth concept to your career journey, one that moves the career conversation beyond the status of "good choice" and into the realm of finding your calling. Let's explore this concept of a calling ... a place where your energy flows from your passion.

4.1: What We Know

A good deal of the literature which pertains to finding your calling can be found in religious or spiritual literature. While this literature base is not for everyone, if it is for you then you might find some faith-based answers in your spiritual community. Likewise, many writings for and by artists reference the concept of finding a calling, pursuing a passion, or following the flow of your energy. So if you are artistically inclined, these phrases may be familiar to you. However, if you have not been exposed to this idea via faith or the arts, there is a possibility that you have not considered it at all. And that would be a shame, because the concept of a calling is a very powerful notion, worthy of consideration as you begin your career journey.

The research tells us that far too many people do not enjoy their chosen careers (Adams, 2014). Let's stop and really think about that for a few minutes ... that is sad and disappointing. But this does not have to be your story, as the research offers us some options for avoiding this outcome. The options focus on finding happiness in our passions and successful work-related flow. Mihaly Csikszentmihalyi (2014) is a positive psychologist whose ideas about finding a calling pertain to his research in vital engagement—a way of being that includes both experiences of flow (enjoyed absorption) and significant meaning. Sounds exactly like what we are discussing right? Being joyfully immersed in an activity with passion and energy flow?

So how can this idea and this research help you find your calling? Csikszentmihalyi found that people who are happy in their careers experienced consistent and prolonged patterns of flow. So if flow is a good predictor of satisfactory work, let's think about it some more. Where have you consistently found that "in the zone" sensation of being so deeply immersed in an activity that you lost your sense of time and self? When have you felt a sense of absorbed enjoyment that just seemed to drive you toward deeper involvement? For example, many novel writers describe a sensation of entering their fictional world while writing and not noticing the passage of time or their own hunger as they become one with the story. We often attribute this feeling to artists, dancers, clergy, etc., but I have a friend who is so fascinated with electrical engineering dilemmas that he has looked up late in the evening to realize that his colleagues have all gone home. They probably called out "goodnight" to him, but he did not hear them from his place of absorption in his engineering specifications. Have you ever felt this swept away in a project? If you have, you have a very important life-calling puzzle piece here.

If you have identified some activities that provide a sense of flow or a calling, remember that the flip side of flow is personal meaning. If some of your flow activities include awesome leisure/hobby activities such as video games, social media, watching vampire movies, you might be wondering if this information is really helpful on your career journey. This is where the concept of meaning comes into play. The activities without meaningful depth often remain as treasured hobbies, but the flow activities which are personally meaningful become the kinds of activities that may be signaling a career calling—the type of career path we will both enjoy and look back on someday with pride because our time was well spent on something that matters to us. Think about that part of a calling too—what sorts of activities leave you feeling as if you are living a good life? When you're older, what might you regret not achieving? What activities leave you feeling like the best possible version of yourself? For example, a doctor, firefighter, or suicide hotline attendant may only save a life a few times in her career, but it is those moments that give depth of meaning during the routine days. What would be a peak moment for you that makes the hours of practice or study meaningful?

4.2: How Do You Figure This Out?

Putting what we know into action, we need to look for places where your moments of flow and your moments of meaning overlap in a way that you perceive that intersection as a potential calling. Think about your responses to the questions above. Where do you find overlap? If you've learned about Venn diagrams, you might even want to draw one with flow activities on one side and meaningful activities on the other. Where the circles overlap in the middle, you will find your joy and your pride ... and perhaps your calling. Need something a bit more structured. How about these activities:

YOUR TURN 4.1

Create Your Passion Board

Ready to explore your passion through a creative activity? Start with a piece of poster board, large paper, or even the side of a cardboard box. In the center, place your name (feel free to use markers, paint, or cut out letters if you are artistic ... or just print the letters in black ink if you are a no-frills sort of person). Now, all around your name, create a collage of images, photos, words, phrases, sayings, stickers, logos, poems, and any other inspirations that appeal to you. (Alternatively, if you are a digital artist, you can create this same inspiration using pinboard tools and apps, but I prefer the smell of glue and the satisfaction of a tactile approach.)

When you look at your passion board, what themes do you see? Do you know why the items you have chosen appeal to you? What emotions do you feel while looking at your board? And now the hard question ... are there jobs/hobbies/careers that might cause you to feel the way you feel when you look at this board? Roles you can hold which feed these passions? Possibilities which might arise from following these passions ... a calling, if you will, instead of just a job? Keep these possibilities in mind as you explore your options. There is something satisfying about finding work or hobbies that you are called to experience. As your awareness of your passions grows, you will become more aware of ways to surround yourself with that which calls to you.

YOUR TURN 4.2

"Let's Play!"

It's a funny thing about growing up. The older we get, the more we are conditioned to overthink things and to try to give the "correct" answer instead of the genuine one. Think about it. When someone says, "Hi. How are you?" do you usually say "Fine, thanks," even if you aren't? And when someone sneezes, do you usually say "Bless you" automatically? Most of us do. So it is no surprise that when someone asks "What is your calling?" we struggle to come up with the right reflexive answer. But here's the thing—there isn't a standard correct answer. We can't really think of this answer traditionally ... we need to feel our way toward it. This is something that was so much easier for us to do as small children, but we became socialized away from our impulses. We pick courses and activities that look good for college admissions, or may earn us cash, or make others proud ... somewhere along the way we stopped playing joyfully. Ready to revisit your childhood? Let's see if your calling is still there ...

Make a list of all the things you loved to do as a child. Reading over that list, do you remember why those activities brought you joy? Do you think you would enjoy that same activity now? (If you are unsure, perhaps you need to try it again and see ... that swing set is calling, crayons are cheap, and that spot under the dining room table is still rather special). So those activities you loved as a child ... what might be some adult equivalents that cause the same joy, energy flow, and/or satisfaction? For example, when I was a child, I loved to write in workbooks ... and now I'm writing this one for you. And Frank Lloyd Wright (the famous architect who built Falling Waters) is said to have spent many hours playing with building blocks as a child (Alofsin, 1993). What do you love most about the positive experiences of your childhood, and what can you learn about your calling from revisiting these memories?

4.3: How Others Use This Information

So this chapter is sometimes a bit more difficult to discuss, as words like passions and energy flow are more difficult to operationally define and discuss. But your journey narrators have done a fabulous job of conveying this elusive phase of the career exploration process.

VOICES FROM CAMPUS 4.1

Kelsey's Corner (A Graduate Student's Perspective)

Oftentimes when people discuss their "calling" it almost seems mythical. A lot of peers I have interacted with have even confused their calling for their dream job. In fact, I still have conversations with one of my friends who believes his calling is to be a professional basketball player. The only problem is he really is mediocre at basketball, by his own admittance. Confusing these two terms can actually be detrimental to your career journey. So if we now know a calling is something we enjoy doing so much that we get lost in the work and is also very meaningful to us, how do we even pinpoint what that is? When I was searching for my calling during my undergraduate career, I was looking into everything but the topic that made sense. All of my human development classes resonated with me. I enjoyed going to class (yes, even at 8 a.m.), and I actually wanted to complete my assignments long before the day they were due. But I just couldn't see that this, counseling and helping people, was my calling. I remember talking to my parents after my first semester in my new major and telling them I had received my first 4.0 GPA. They were very proud of me, but they still asked the dreaded question, "Well maybe you aren't challenging yourself, do you think it's too easy?" This question used to anger me to no end. Of course it was easy! This is what I am good at; this is my calling! Why should I pick a career that challenges me past the level of learning and into the level of frustration and resentment? I knew my parents had good intentions, so I politely declined their sentiments and continued down the path towards what I still believe to this day is my calling. Yes, it's easy and yes, sometimes it's challenging, but most of all I am so good at it, I'm passionate about it, and I truly feel as though I am making a difference in the lives of many individuals. The moral of my story is, don't eliminate something as your calling that has meaning to you solely because it's easy, you're just teeming with flow.

VOICES FROM CAMPUS 4.2

Rebekah's Voice (A New Professional's Perspective)

Although I did grow up in a religious household, after coming out and having some negative responses, I lost touch with my faith. Although my faith faded away, the idea and concept of a calling still resonated with me in college. I wanted to do something meaningful with my life—something I could look back on and feel proud about. I mentioned earlier that one of my skills is listening. I also enjoy and am good at helping people. As I approached my last year in college I was standing at a fork in the road. Do I apply for jobs or do I apply for graduate school? As a previous self-doubter I thought to myself "I'm not smart enough to go to graduate school." Luckily, I had some encouragement from some professors and a mentor who assured me of my ability to get accepted to graduate school in a helping profession field.

Finding your calling may be easier than you think. For me, this fourth prong was the easiest to figure out. I get excited when I'm able to help someone, and I enjoy listening to people talk about their lives. When I'm in these moments, I lose track of time. I get invested in helping them, and I enjoy seeing them become successful and strive despite their struggles. That is also one of the reasons, when I was asked to be a campus voice for this book, that I jumped on the opportunity. Although we may never meet, knowing that my experiences and words of encouragement (at least I hope they encourage you) are helping you find your way and figure out your path gives me great joy, and writing these sections doesn't feel like "work" because of it. When you are working, but it doesn't feel like you are working, then you are on the right track to finding YOUR calling.

4.4: How You Can Use This Information

Excellent work on completing the first four chapters in this section. Now that you have your unique combination of puzzle pieces, you are ready to put all those pieces together and see what career picture is forming. Chapter 5 will walk you through the process of assembling your puzzle and beginning to truly understand where you might fit in the world of work.

4.5: Want More?

Don't forget that you have more opportunities to explore in the "Where to Turn" appendices at the end of this book, where you will find resources *In Print, On the Web,* and *On Campus.*

4.6: The Take Away

- This chapter deviates a bit from the more pragmatic chapters in this career workbook, and no, we can't all be poets, dancers, and rock stars ... but we can be optimistically realistic and hope that we can make a living doing what we love.

- Paying careful attention to our passions, energy flow, and personal meaning making can be as valuable as assessing values, interests, and skills ... some might even say more valuable if we are finding our calling instead of just looking for a job.

References

Adams, S. (2014, June 20). Most Americans are unhappy at work. Forbes. Retrieved from http://www.forbes.com/sites/susanadams/2014/06/20/most-americans-are-unhappy-at-work/#4a4698375862

Alofsin, A. (1993). *Frank Lloyd Wright the lost years, 1910–1922: A study of influence.* Chicago: University of Chicago Press.

Csikszentmihalyi, M. (2014). *Flow and the foundations of positive psychology: The collected works of Mihaly Csikszentmihalyi.* New York: Springer.

Winfrey, O. (2014). *What I know for sure.* Chicago: Flatiron Books.

ASSEMBLING YOUR PUZZLE

WHAT PICTURE IS FORMING?

Who in the world am I? Ah, that's the great puzzle.

—Lewis Carroll, Alice in Wonderland

A s you complete this first unit, you have the pieces of the puzzle you need to see your unique and personal career calling taking shape. At this point, you have explored your unique qualities/ values, interests, aptitudes/skills, and passions. But like any puzzle, even when the box contains all the pieces, there is still some time and effort required to assemble those pieces into a meaningful picture. Chapter 5 will walk you through the process of assembling your puzzle and beginning to truly understand where you might fit in the world of work. In many ways, this might be the chapter you've been waiting for. Ready?

5.1: What We Know

There are numerous modern theories of career development which emphasize personal experience and the right of each individual to construct a meaningful career path that fits personal beliefs, perspectives, and unique worldview. Some of these are more narrative approaches which hold that career paths don't really just "unfold" as described by some traditional approaches, but rather career paths are constructed by the choices you make along the way. In other words, many emerging career professionals believe that the choices you make express your self-concept and move you in a direction in line with the goals that you may not even be fully aware of yet. From these new perspectives on career, you are in charge of your career path. Or to continue our metaphor, you need to put together your own puzzle, because only you will recognize the picture which is forming. That being said, there are still valuable tools which have stood the test of time in helping you to crystallize your career decisions as you consider your options.

When it comes to making sense of where we fit in the world of work, one name appears in the literature again and again: John Holland (Nauta, 2010). Has anyone ever mentioned Holland Codes, RIASEC, or O*Net to you? All of these are derived from the work of John Holland who identified 720 types of people and created a way to categorize them into differing combinations of six basic types: Realistic (Doers), Investigative (Thinkers), Artistic (Creators), Social (Helpers), Enterprising (Persuaders), and Conventional (Organizers).

5.2: How Do You Figure This Out?

Holland Codes have been used to organize both areas of study (your potential college majors) and the world of work (your potential careers). While no system is foolproof, the Holland Codes do provide us with a common language to link our types with both areas of study and future careers, where others who share similar traits and interests have been drawn. Want to give it a try? You can ask your school counselor or career counselor to give an inventory which will produce your Holland Codes (such as the Self-Directed Search (SDS), Vocational Preference Inventory (VPI), Career Aptitude and Strategies Inventory (CASI), Environmental Identity Scale (EIS), or Position Classification Inventory(PCI)). Or if you are a do-it-yourself-er, you can access a free online version at http://personality-testing.info/tests/RIASEC/ from the Open Source Psychometrics Project, or a more simple version at https://www.truity.com/test/holland-code-career-test.

YOUR TURN 5.1

A Quick and Easy Holland Theme Exercise

In addition to the formal assessments which yield your Holland Code, you may also select your own codes based on the descriptions. Read through each of these six Holland theme descriptions of people, interests, and skills. In the spaces at the bottom, write the names of the three themes that you believe describe you the best in order (first, second, and third best descriptions). You might also want to highlight the words that best describe you in each description.

R	REALISTIC	Do you have athletic or mechanical ability? Do you prefer to work with objects, machines, tools, plants, or animals, or to be outdoors?
I	INVESTIGATIVE	Do you like to observe, learn, investigate, analyze, evaluate, or solve problems?
A	ARTISTIC	Do you have artistic, innovating, or intuitional abilities? Do you like to work in unstructured situations, using your imagination or creativity?
S	SOCIAL	Do you like to work with people to inform, enlighten, help, train, develop, or cure them? Are you skilled with words?
E	ENTERPRISING	Do you like to work with people—influencing, persuading, leading, or managing them for organizational goals or for economic gain?

C	CONVENTIONAL	Do you like to work with data? Do you have clerical or numerical ability? Do you like to carry things out in detail or follow through on others' instructions?

Which three (in order) describe you best?

1. _____ 2. _____ 3. _____

Adapted from Holland, J. L. (1997). *Making vocational choices: A theory of vocational personalities and work environments* (3rd ed.). Odessa, FL: Psychological Assessment Resources.

YOUR TURN 5.2

Seeing Yourself Through a Friend's Eyes

So far you have worked to understand yourself better so you can find your career calling. But if you aren't quite there yet, how about a second opinion? Sometimes the view from the outside has some worthwhile perspectives which help us fill in that big picture. Maybe it's time to ask a trusted friend to fill in what you might have missed. So sit with a friend and try this exercise:

1. Ask your friend to name three of your strengths.

   _____

   _____

   _____

   _____

   _____

2. Tell your friend about one of your interests or passions and ask if that is in line with the outside perspective? If not, ask about what you are perceived to be interested in or passionate about.

    _____

    _____

    _____

    _____

    _____

3. Now ... here is where your friend gets to be creative. Ask your friend to tell an imaginary story of your life based on the interest(s)/passion(s) and strengths. (For instance, "I've noticed that you are warm, friendly, and motivated to succeed. You said your passion is for baking, but I've always thought of you as someone who is most passionate about dogs. So I see you opening this trendy dog treat bakery in a warm little coastal town. You are greeting all of your customers (both human and canine) with a big warm smile and the sign over the door says "Welcome to the Barkery." Your specialties of the day are Pug Loaf Slices and Beagle Bites.) Let's see how your friend does:

    _____

    _____

    _____

    _____

    _____

4. Okay ... go ahead and roll with this scenario. What if this really were your life? Can you explain to your friend all that appeals to you about this imaginary future? ("I really love the idea of playing around with creative dog treats and making signboards that have punny dog specials. And hey ... thanks for putting me by the ocean—I didn't know you knew that about me.) But also tell your friend what makes you cringe about this

story ("I don't think I would ever want to run my own business. I think I want a small dependable salary and plenty of time off to spend with my family. I think I want to work for someone else.")

_____

_____

_____

_____

_____

5. Okay, if your friend is still willing to play along, ask for a story revision. ("Well then, take two … You work for a prestigious café in a wealthy dog-loving seaside town. The café has outdoor seating where patrons are welcome to bring their pets. You have been hired to create daily specials which mimic the offerings for humans, but are nutritionally balanced for canines. You create these items and fill the doggie cases three mornings per week, which leaves you plenty of time to write your canine cookbook and care for your family.") Round Two:

_____

_____

_____

_____

_____

6. Keep this process going back and forth for a few rounds until the story feels right (or until your friend gets bored with it all and wants to eat). This may take a few more rounds, but hopefully your friend will suggest some unexpected scenarios that force you to think outside of any box you may have accidentally created for yourself. Try not to let any knee-jerk negativity squelch the creative flow. (Avoid saying, "No one would pay me to do that" or "Where would I get the money to start that?") This exercise is about learning how someone else would creatively combine

your unique qualities into opportunities tailored to your strengths. Let it flow playfully and see what shakes loose. Try not to stop until the story feels completely satisfying. You've just shaped your passion into something tangible and helped define what you do and do not want for your calling. Sometimes we really do get by with a little help from our friends. Try again:

_____

_____

_____

_____

_____

5.3: How Others Use This Information

For this chapter, your storytellers will recap and explain how they put all their pieces together to form portraits of themselves that looked like their future. They will share with you those moments of clarity when the puzzle came together and they liked what they saw.

VOICES FROM CAMPUS 5.1

Kelsey's Corner (A Graduate Student's Perspective)

From the first day of preschool to the first day of college, we are consistently asked what we want to do when we grow up. Unfortunately, many college students never find the answer to this question and end up settling for a career that means nothing to them. For me, this journey to finding my path was a classic case of trial and error. I started with my interests, scheduling my first semester of college around cool topics. To no surprise, not all of those cool classes turned out to be my cup of tea so to speak. During my second semester I tried to narrow down my classes to what I was interested in and good at. This decision led to me changing my major three times between my freshman year and last semester of my sophomore year. This was an exciting and terrifying time for me. The closer I got to finding my niche, the happier I was. At the same time, the more I changed my major, the more I felt lost in my own world. During my junior year, I was forced to think about life after graduation. I loved my major, and its focus was so broad that I could really apply for any job that dealt with human development. Um, hello—that's practically anything because we are all humans continuing to develop. As I thought about what I could do, I repeatedly came back to academics and school. That's when it hit me. Who said I had to leave academics? School had always been my niche, my forte. So I got to it; I researched all careers in the education system and I found school counseling. School AND helping people? This was the best thing ever, for me at least. Reaching that realization and making that decision was the last piece of my puzzle. I have now received my Masters of Education and certification in school counseling. If I didn't take the time to find this, if I ran away and took the easy way out, I would have settled miserably. Take it from me, your average stranger with similar experiences, and in fear of sounding too cliché, the easy way isn't always the right way. So what are you waiting for? Go finish your own puzzle!

VOICES FROM CAMPUS 5.2

Rebekah's Voice (A New Professional's Perspective)

After I applied to graduate school for social work (the helping profession I chose), I awaited acceptance letters. I only applied to three schools, but I was offered admission to all three. Long story short, I accepted at an institution in Boston and over the summer everything went wrong. I couldn't find housing, I wasn't selected for the internship I interviewed for, and because of traffic I missed a very important appointment to talk about financial aid and couldn't reschedule for the same day. I thought to myself, maybe this is the universe telling me Boston is not right. So I contacted the school in Pennsylvania (where I was currently located) and asked if I could accept their admission offer although I had already declined it and they said yes. Finding housing in the new area was easy. I met with two different people renting rooms and in one day I had a place to stay.

After moving to the new town, I applied for a job and started working immediately and classes started in just a few weeks. In late October, I found myself really struggling in the program, not connecting with any of my classmates, and I was floundering with my emotions about it all. I decided it would be best to withdraw from the program. After withdrawing I met with my mentor (the same one who assured me I'm smart enough for graduate school) and told her about the situation. We discussed my involvement in the LGBTQA program and she looked at me and said "You know you could be a professional LGBTQA leader, right?" and that was my "Aha!" moment. I thought, "Duh, Rebekah" but it never dawned on me. She encouraged me to apply for the higher education counseling and student affairs program in which she taught.

In the next few weeks I received my offer letter and told a friend of mine, who I met as an orientation leader and who started the program the semester before, that I'd be joining her. She told me of an open graduate assistantship and I met with the director of the department and was hired for that as well. The assistantship offered on-campus housing, so moving back was easy. I graduated two years later with my Master's degree and landed my first job right away doing LGBTQ+ work at a university.

Did you notice that the final puzzle piece I picked up didn't fit? And the one after that didn't fit either. My puzzle had extra pieces. And yours might too. And if it does, remember that even if you have extra pieces in your box, the right one is still there waiting for you to put it into place. Trust yourself that you will find the right one.

5.4: How You Can Use This Information

Now that you have completed the first section of this book, "Your Career Calling is Personal: Who Are You?," you have probably figured out some interesting things about yourself. Some people might want to take a break here, reflect a bit more, and fine-tune their career picture. That is a great idea. Why not skim back over the activities you have completed and talk about what you have learned with someone you trust. And when you are truly ready to move on again, you can begin the second section entitled "Your Career Dovetails With the World: Where Do You Fit?" which will help you explore your resources, opportunities, and challenges as you match your self-knowledge with the world around you. So keep reading … the exciting part of this project is just starting.

5.5: Want More?

Don't forget that you have more opportunities to explore in the "Where to Turn" appendices at the end of this book, where you will find resources *In Print, On the Web,* and *On Campus.*

5.6: The Take Away

- Your calling begins with moments of clarity where the pieces fit together and a meaningful future seems not only possible, but probable.

- Sometimes we find our individuation from others by first understanding what we have in common.

References

Carroll, L. (2006). *Alice's adventures in wonderland.* New York, NY: Bantam Dell. (Original work published 1865).

Holland, J. L. (1997). *Making vocational choices: A theory of vocational personalities and work environments* (3rd ed.). Odessa, FL: Psychological Assessment Resources.

Nauta, M. (2010). The development, evolution, and status of Holland's Theory of Vocational Personalities: Reflections and future directions for counseling psychology. *Journal of Counseling Psychology, 57*(1), 11–22.

UNIT II:
YOUR CAREER
DOVETAILS WITH
THE WORLD: WHERE
DO YOU FIT?

IDENTIFYING YOUR RESOURCES

WHAT MORE DO YOU NEED TO BEGIN YOUR JOURNEY?

It takes a village to … launch an adult!

Now that you have identified a potential career path or two, it is time to start figuring out how to make this happen. It is all too easy to procrastinate and let your career aspirations float indefinitely in the land of maybe someday with all the other dreams and what ifs. But to start actualizing your career path, you will need to start taking stock of your resources. What support, opportunities, and resources do you already have and what more do you need for this journey? It is no secret that some young people start the journey with more resources than others. If you have the benefit of free time, financial support, caring family and friends, higher intellect, gifts and talents, etc., then you are on your way! But realistically, most of us do not have all of these things—we need to cultivate and improve upon our situation before we begin, and that is okay. You can do this even if things do not always flow easily in your direction. You can take an honest look at your resources and figure out ways to improve your opportunities by increasing your resources. Let's get started.

6.1: What We Know

It is certainly no secret that students who use all available resources find them-selves on a smoother path. Over the years, studies have found that students who utilize school/campus resources such as counseling, guidance, career planning and placement, tutoring, mentoring, writing and math labs, and other academic and social support services are better positioned for success (Kuh, 2005; O'Gara, Mechur Karp, & Hughes, 2009). I could list the studies here and go on for several pages with data, but I think the important message from the literature for you is that you do not need to already have all the resources you need for success. Some employers provide on-the-job training, appren-ticeship models, and compensation for continuing education. Most colleges and universities provide programs for financial, academic, social, and cultural support to varying degrees. So if you assess the resources you already have and find them lacking, don't despair. Instead, use this book, including the appendices, the Internet, and your high school counselors to find additional resources which can help you set out on your journey.

6.2: How You Can Use This Information

One of your most valuable resources is the relationships you have with other human beings who are on your side and willing to support you as you embark on your career journey. Certainly, my opinion here is biased, as expanding and deepening relationships is the heart of the work that I do as a counselor. But I truly believe that the wider the network of people who care about you, the more likely it is that you will have a successful career journey, as none of us were meant to do this all alone. The quality of your personal relationships affects the richness of your personal vision, your hope for the future, and the sense that you can really make it happen. So it is a good time to take stock of your circle of support as a resource for your career journey.

YOUR TURN 6.1

What Does Your Circle of Support Look Like?

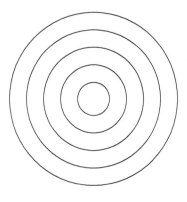

If you are standing in the center circle of this diagram, the ring of support around you is your very closest family and friends. The next ring is your extended circle of family, casual friends, and neighbors. The next circle is folks you know from school and work. The final circle is community members and professionals. Though they are grouped around you in order of closeness of relationship, ALL of the individuals in these circles can support you.

1. Who are the people in your first ring of support? Your closest family members and friends? These are the people who are closest to you and know you best. These are people you can't imagine living without. They're often your immediate family and best friends. Can you list these people below? Use more room if needed.

    _____

    _____

    _____

    _____

    _____

2. Who are the people in your second ring of support? Your extended circle of family and casual friends? These are your extended family members, casual friends, neighbors, and people who know you through activities, such as your house of worship, clubs, or other organizations to which you belong. These are people who also care about you and share common interests with you. Can you list these people below? Use more room if needed.

    _____

    _____

    _____

    _____

    _____

3. Who are the people in your third ring of support? Your third ring is your school and/or work contacts. This group might include your classmates, teachers, coaches, advisors, co-workers, or supervisors. These are the people who may not feel emotionally close to you, and yet they are in a position to see you from an outside perspective and offer you feedback and encouragement based on their observations of you in academic and professional settings. Their support can be

invaluable. Can you list some of these people below? Use more room if needed.

_____

_____

_____

_____

_____

4. Who are the people in your fourth ring of support? Your fourth ring consists of community members and professional helpers or service providers. These people know you because of their professional interactions with you. They might be service providers like counselors, trainers, nurses, police officers, librarians, or bus drivers. These are the people who accepted the responsibility of providing services to you in your community. They may not come immediately to mind as supportive, but each can provide you with a different opportunity to move forward, if you trust them to be part of your journey. When you cross paths with these individuals, perhaps you should tell them what you hope to accomplish. Can you list a few of these people below? Use more room if needed.

_____

_____

_____

_____

_____

I probably don't have to tell you that another resource you will need is the means to pursue your dream. Advanced training, technical school, college, graduate school, etc. all have a cost. That cost can be largely financial, but it can also involve time, energy, giving up other activities, and giving up the familiar for the unknown. It can even cost you your health or sense of well-being if you don't attend to your self-care as your pursue your dream. So what resources do you have now as you get ready to begin? Consider the obvious resources such as time, money, and background education/training, but also consider other factors like the traits/gifts you have up your sleeve and the opportunities available to you if you succeed. Let's take stock of what you have as you begin your journey.

YOUR TURN 6.2

"Head West ... Opportunities Await You!"

If you've paid attention to your history books (or are a fan of Laura Ingalls Wilder) then you know that many people used to load up their belongings onto a Conestoga wagon and head west in search of new opportunities. If you imagine your career journey as a similar adventure, then take the metaphor a bit further and ask yourself if the wheels on the wagon are strong enough to support your journey? (Or if you prefer to look forward instead of back with your metaphor, is your starship strong enough to support you as you boldly go where you have never gone before?)

If you are the hub of this wagon wheel, imagine that the eight spokes are resources you need for your journey. Can you journal on and/or initiate a discussion with a trusted other about the current state of each spoke? Which ones are strong enough for the journey? Which are weak or broken and need repair or replacement? If your wagon wheel is not ready to journey too far west, how far do you think you can go with the resources you have now? How can you acquire more resources?

Spoke #1:   Financial Resources

Spoke #2:   Skills (Academic and/or Work Related)

Spoke #3:   Intellect, Talent, Knowledge, Gifts in Line With Goals

Spoke #4:   Motivation to Try

Spoke #5:   Determination to Succeed

Spoke #6:   Time to Commit to your Goal

Spoke #7:   Physical/Emotional Strength for the Journey

Spoke #8:   Foreseeable Opportunities in Your Future

6.3: How Can Professionals Help?

Taking stock of your resources can be quite stressful, especially if your tally is low. But do not let that discourage you. There are resources you do not know about yet. Your school or college counselors often have greater insight into nontraditional ways to plan, pay for, and build a support network. They know about programs, scholarships, individuals, foundations, and opportunities that you can access to help you succeed. Please do not be tempted to throw in the towel if the road ahead looks bumpy and difficult. I strongly encourage you to use the services of professional counselors and advisors to explore at this stage and to never decide you can't do it if you haven't yet consulted with a professional helper.

6.4: How Others Use This Information

As in the previous chapters, two people have generously agreed to share how they navigated this phase, because they both hope that reading about their twists and turns will help you as you take stock of a phase that often feels like two steps forward and one back.

VOICES FROM CAMPUS 6.1

Kelsey's Corner (A Graduate Student's Perspective)

In terms of resources, I have always been pretty privileged, particularly throughout my journey of attaining my career goals. For starters, my parents financially contributed to my education, which in my case was a very large aspect of my aspirations. Note here that I did not say they completely financially supported me through my education, rather they contributed. An enormous privilege, yes, but I did still have to work throughout my entire education which was a bummer and very time consuming. Second, I was privileged to have support from my mother in particular, whose career was in the same field that I was pursuing; she understood the struggles and successes that seemed unimportant to someone not in a human services field. Third, and more importantly in my opinion, I found support in my university, my community at the time. After meeting with my college advisor and deciding to switch my major, she provided me with a ton of resources on campus to help further develop my path. The resources included on-campus tutoring, how to find office hours for my professors, and most helpful to me, a list of clubs and societies specifically for my major and corresponding academic college. Even though I was a little nervous to meet new people in my major, I pushed myself to go to the club meetings (yes, I found time between studying, work, and keeping a social life). This was the best thing I ever did for my journey. I was able to relate to similar struggles, discuss common classes and assignments, make new friends, and thus expand my support network. This was a crazy concept to me, because it was so simple. But I guess famous fashion designer Carolina Herrera was right, "sometimes the simplest things are the most profound."

VOICES FROM CAMPUS 6.2

Rebekah's Voice (A New Professional's Perspective)

I never realized until recently that I am a first-generation college student. I think because I come from a middle-class family, I thought I had "too much" of an advantage when it came to my resources. Although my family didn't struggle financially on a day-to-day basis, after I filled out my first FAFSA and it told me what my family was expected to contribute, I started to panic. I used my high school counselor as a resource. She shared with me some different scholarship opportunities my high school offered and encouraged me to check out national organizations too. I found some applications for scholarships I thought I could win, and some I thought I couldn't, and applied for all of them. I did receive some, for which I was grateful.

My other concern when applying for college was my SAT scores. They were not acceptable; part of that is because I'm not the greatest test taker, and part is because my visual disability causes my eyes to get fatigued, which affects my concentration. So I used my high school teachers to write letters of recommendation stating that I work hard and get good grades. Since my SAT scores didn't represent my ability to succeed in college, I had people who could assure the colleges I'd be successful.

As I mentioned in a previous chapter, I applied for graduate school in social work even though I was not a social work major as an undergraduate. In order to feel confident in my applications, I reached out to a social work professor who I knew from a committee we worked on and she also wrote a letter stating that I had the potential to succeed in the profession even though I lacked the undergraduate knowledge of social work.

Although my resources appear to have been mostly people, there were others as well and, in my job, currently I use the Internet all the time. And if I didn't have a computer, my local library has them I can use them for free. It may seem like you don't have resources, but you really do! This book itself is a resource for you and each chapter provides resources. Don't be afraid to ask for help and remember to believe in yourself.

6.5: How You Can Use This Information

Now that you have completed this chapter and have a better understanding of all the resources available to you, you are encouraged to move on to Chapter 7, where you will begin to explore your opportunities and develop a process for weighing the costs and benefits of you potential career paths.

6.6: Want More?

Don't forget that you have more opportunities to explore in the "Where to Turn" appendices at the end of this book, where you will find resources *In Print, On the Web,* and *On Campus.*

6.7: The Take Away

- Moving from the dream to the reality will be smoother if you stockpile resources for the journey.

- There are people ready to help you launch forward, so you just need to be ready and willing to invite them into your plan.

References

Kuh, G. D. (2005). Promoting student success: What campus leaders can do. Occasional Paper No. 1. National Survey of Student Engagement.

O'Gara, L., Mechur Karp, M., & Hughes, K. L. (2009). Student success courses in the community college: An exploratory study of student perspectives. *Community College Review, 36*(3), 195–218.

EVALUATING YOUR OPPORTUNITIES

WHAT IS THE COST/BENEFIT OF YOUR POTENTIAL PATHS?

Be careful not to compromise what you want most for what you want now.

—Zig Ziglar

L et's begin by acknowledging that many individuals are looking for a career that will pay well. It would be naïve to pretend that finding your career calling is a process which does not include salary expectations. Some of us are comfortable with a lower salary and some are willing to accept a smaller paycheck for other rewards such as strong benefits packages, exciting and rewarding work, fame or appreciation of our work, autonomy in the workplace, and many other desirable aspects. That being said, the cost of living an adult life is what it is, and after Chapter 6 you may have decided that you do not have the resources necessary to let salary take the back seat. So in this chapter, we will explore the delicate balance between opportunities that pay now and those that require patience and early investment of resources without immediate gain.

7.1: What We Know

There was a time when a discussion regarding the cost of college usually centered upon the decision to go to college or to go straight into the workforce, and the arguments weighed heavily in favor of a college education leading to a higher lifetime salary. I believe these arguments are still valid, but the issue is more complicated given the rising costs of a college education and the saturation of certain fields with new graduates. Some convincing arguments these days focus as much on the developmental advantages of a college experience as they do on salary potential. In fact, I have heard college referred to as the "new high school experience," referring to the fact that college seems to be more of an expectation than an option (Rosenbaum, 2001). When we speak about OPPORTUNITY for anyone to attend, I applaud this change, but if the conversation moves toward OBLIGATION for everyone to attend, I am less enthusiastic. I am going to make the unpopular declaration that a traditional residential four-year college experience beginning at age 18 is not for everyone. There are many, many paths that include part-time attendance, two-year colleges, attending at a more mature age, and living off campus or at home. There is also the traditional option of entering the workforce directly in a family business, apprenticeship model, or career not requiring advanced education. Of course we also need to consider options outside of this discussion, such as military service, artistic/creative paths, dot-com startups, day trading, new and creative entrepreneurial endeavors, and other alternative paths paved by millennials. But all this being said, an argument that seems to capture the zeitgeist has been fueled by Mike Rowe, a television and Internet voice who is asking us to dialogue about the skills gap. Mike Rowe and plenty of others are concerned that we have devalued the skilled trades in favor of a college education for everyone. Indeed, Gardner's multiple intelligence theories (Gardner, 2011) lead us to believe that people find their callings using different assets, and for those who enjoy working with their hands and being more active, the skilled trades might be a great match. So if you like to read or listen to podcasts or enter the dialogue, it is a fascinating topic. But what I want you to hear is this: all of these options are on the table for you, and only you can determine if the cost of education is compatible with your career goals. If you are thinking of a different path, you'll also need to analyze the potential long-term outcome of other choices as well. Whatever you choose, try to determine if the outcome is worth the cost, both financially and personally.

Whether you are seeking scholarships for traditional higher education, a mikeroweWORKS scholarship in the trades, or other funding opportunities such as work-study programs, jobs that reimburse educational expenses for employees, military ROTC, or grants and loans, you will need to complete a Free Application for Federal Student Aid (FAFSA) (https://fafsa.ed.gov/) for your higher education financial aid division to process your aid.

While you are pursuing education, you may be advised to consider cooperative education, internships, summer and/or part-time jobs, and volunteer experiences. Whether these pay well, a little, or not at all, you will need to balance your immediate needs for cash with your longer term needs to develop the right set of skills and experiences that will help you move along your identified career path. I have no easy advice for you here, as everyone is in a different situation based on resources and opportunities. But let's look at some of your options.

Cooperative education (co-op) is a combination of an academic experience for credit related and outside work experience. If you decide to co-op, you will be able to gain credits for your work experience. Cooperative education is usually a carefully alternated series of academic experience with work experiences which are generally both paid and intended to advance the education of the student in a desired career path. It has its benefits, especially in a high school setting. But remember that in a college setting, you will be paying tuition for the experience if you are receiving credit for it.

Internships, both paid and unpaid, are highly related to a chosen career path and plan of study. They often come toward the end of your studies and can be a bridge to the world of work and a fabulous networking opportunity. Internships are often encouraged for those who have the necessary resources, such as transportation, appropriate clothing, and endorsements from faculty.

Summer or part-time jobs are obviously paid positions which can solve immediate needs for money, but they are often unrelated to the career path. If you must work your way through your education, try to find a way to incorporate what you learn at each job into a transferable skills list which you can discuss in your cover letter or on a job interview. You might be surprised by how much you can learn about yourself and your strengths while serving tables, assisting customers, and caring for children. As my Nanny always told me, honest hard work builds character ... and your bank account.

Volunteer experience is usually unpaid, but hopefully related to your interests. The rewards of completing volunteer work are many and varied and can be an opportunity to discover how much you have to give. It can be a way of experiencing your own power to help and potential to succeed. Sometimes, volunteer work can even be an unexpected opportunity to consider a different career path, if you find a new passion while volunteering. Unfortunately, the unpaid nature of volunteering means that some students just can't fit it in with a paying job and studies. But if your resources permit you to contribute some of your time, volunteerism can help you realize your personal and professional potential while providing you with an opportunity to meet the needs of others and network for yourself. So what do you think? Would you like to grow through volunteerism?

7.2: How You Can Use This Information

Beginning the process of deciding what education, training, and opportunities are right for you is an intimidating task. I don't advise you to make these choices alone. They require careful consideration and knowledge of yourself and your goals. I hope you are finding this book helpful in learning about yourself, but at this stage you will need to begin researching your options, hopefully with a trusted other. There are many helpful worksheets on the Web, and your counselors probably have some as well, but here is one activity to start the process.

YOUR TURN 7.1

Considering Your Educational Options

As you begin to investigate and narrow down your choices, you will want to answer some questions candidly for yourself. Please journal on these questions and/or discuss them with a trusted other.

1. Do you want to continue your education? When?

2. Why do you want to go to college?

3. What abilities do you want to hone or develop?

4. How can further education help you reach your career (or personal) goals?

5. Compare your life with and without further education. In each scenario, where might you be in 5 years? 10 years? 20 years?

6. What kind of further education interests you?

    Type?

        Four-year prep for advanced degree?

        Four-year terminal?

        Two-year/community college then transfer?

        Two-year/community college then enter workforce?

        Trade or vocational school?

        Other?

        Public? Private? Specialized?

    Location?

        Geographic region?

        Urban? Suburban? Rural?

        Outside the United States?

        Climate?

        Distance from home?

    Size?

        Large? (20,000+)

        Medium? (10,000+)

        Small? (under 10,000)

    Residential Life?

        Campus traditional housing?

        Campus apartment?

        Greek letter housing?

Off-campus apartment or house?

Live at home and commute?

Cost/Financial Aid?

What is your maximum family contribution?

_____

Is financial aid essential to attend?

No?

Yes, partial okay?

Yes, full aid needed?

Other needs? Transportation?

Campus health/counseling?

Disability support? LGBTQ support?

Cultural support?

Bridge program?

Sports?

Clubs?

Tutorial support?

Ready to get into the details even further? Visit http://www.collegeview.com/collegesearch/index.jsp.

If two individuals with the same diploma/degree and the same GPA apply for the same job, but one has a related experience, who do you think will most likely get the position? The answer is usually the person with the most experience, but here is where it gets tricky. Some of us are better at explaining how our experiences would be helpful in the new job. For example, if two people are being considered for the same position at a tech company, but one (call her Desiree) has an unpaid internship at a major corporation, most folks would assume that Desiree would get the position because she has the related experience. But wait, not so fast. What if the other applicant (call her Julia) worked several unrelated part-time jobs to pay her way through school. Some folks would say Julia would not get the position, but in reality, it might come down to Julia's ability to articulate what she learned from those jobs and how she plans to bring those skills to the tech position. If Julia is well prepared and has kept track of what she has learned from every job she held, every club/team/group she led, and every opportunity to grow she has seized, she just might be the one hired. I bet, like Julia, you may have more transferable skills than you realize. Remember this example when you are faced with difficult decisions about opportunities that pay (paid jobs and paid internships) and opportunities that do not pay (volunteerism) or even cost you to participate (higher education and co-ops). Think carefully and creatively about the costs and benefits of these various opportunities in light of your specific situation. Perhaps you can begin by logging your development through each opportunity, so that you can explain your growth to potential employers down the road.

YOUR TURN 7.2

In an effort to make every opportunity work in your favor, consider keeping a journal or log of your growth for every opportunity you have—certainly for any jobs you have (paid or unpaid), but also for any leadership roles you hold and for anything you do that gives you a way to grow.

- What was my job, task, or role? (What skills or qualities were necessary for it?)

- What did I learn here? (What do I know now that I wish I had known before I started?)

- How did I grow in this experience? (How am I different now than I was before the experience?)

- What did I accomplish in this role? (If I were to receive recognition for some aspect of my performance here, what would the award be for?)

- How would I speak about this to a potential employer someday? (How would I explain the value of my experience as it pertains to skills and qualities I now have which can benefit my future employers/co-workers/clients/profession?)

7.3: How Can Professionals Help?

At this phase, I once again refer you to school counselors and higher education counselors. More specifically, this may be a good time to begin speaking with a financial aid officer and/or a career planning and placement counselor. And since this step involves finances, you will need to work with your parents (especially if you are still their dependent) and/or your spouse (if applicable) to complete the FAFSA and discuss what they may or may not be able to contribute to your education.

7.4: How Others Use This Information

Once again, our campus voice writers are sharing their experiences with you so you can see how all of these choices can lead to concrete steps in your journey. Both of your journey writers chose higher education, but I encourage you to speak to individuals who chose a different path so you can weigh your options.

Kelsey's Corner (A Graduate Student's Perspective)

The difficult decision between money or experience was always a battle for me. It is not often in human services that you will find a paid internship due to funding, or lack thereof. I wanted the experience because all I heard through high school and college was to get into my field through related research as soon as possible to build my résumé. Yeah, that sounds easy except for the fact that I was also a broke college student and still needed to do things like eat and have clean clothes. So I was faced with this necessary and completely mind-numbing decision: Do I work on campus in the dining commons so I can grocery shop and go to the movies with my friends or do I dedicate my free time to research in my major so I can beef up my résumé? Simply (well, in hindsight it seems simple), I did both. I found a research lab that understood I also needed to work, so they put me on for only 10 unpaid hours per week of research. And guess what, I also found a job on campus working at a bistro who similarly understood that I needed to work on my educational opportunities, so I worked 10 paid hours per week there. It was tough, trust me, but it was something I had to do. After that challenging year of real-life choices, I started to look for opportunities that would somewhat relate to my field but also pay. The following year I was a resident assistant for first-year students. This was a HUGE commitment. I mean come on, I was literally living with freshmen … 37 of them on a co-ed floor. And they looked to me for guidance! I started knocking things off my "need so I can live" list: Bedroom, Check! Meal plan, Check! Earplugs, Check (okay, you wouldn't think this is a necessity to live but put yourself in my shoes as a senior living with freshmen)! Then I started relating it to counseling, which it obviously did. Best of both worlds if you ask me. Once I knew what to look for and realized it didn't have to be a this-OR-that situation, opportunities seemed to be coming up out of nowhere. So I guess the moral of the story is that keeping an open mind can make things seem less complicated.

VOICES FROM CAMPUS 7.2

Rebekah's Voice (A New Professional's Perspective)

After I changed my major to sociology and women's & gender studies, the question I received immediately after "What are you going to do with that?" was "How are you going to make money?" This idea that money is the most important thing really bothered me. I asked myself, would I rather make a lot of money but hate my job or make a little less money but love my job? Although I know I need money to survive, I went with option B—love my job!

When I was in college, I did need to work, but I found an on-campus job as a desk assistant (DA) in Residence Life and the hours were about 8-10 per week depending on the semester, but the major perk was the desk was not staffed by a DA after 6:00 p.m., which gave me ample time to go to the library to study. I also looked for summer jobs. I became an orientation leader (OL) and one thing we always said was "You don't become an OL to make money." We became OLs for the experience! I took the small pay I was given and saved it in order to help provide for myself in the upcoming fall. At my institution, you could be an OL for more than one year—so I did it for four! And then after I graduated, they offered me a summer position as an orientation staff member. This experience was paid and gave me great transferable skills.

While I was in graduate school, I had to complete practicum and internships which were all unpaid. But as I mentioned in Chapter 5, I was offered a graduate assistantship which paid my tuition and gave me housing and a meal plan! This gave me the opportunity to focus on my studies, make some money, and still gain experience within my field since Residence Life is still an area of higher education.

I say all of this to emphasize that this decision doesn't need to be an either/or situation. It can be a both/and situation if you can find the right opportunities. Be sure to use the resources you listed in Chapter 6 to help you find some of those opportunities that may pay AND give you great experience. Your high school counselor or the career center at your college can help you with this decision and with finding the opportunities available to you. No matter what though, you need to enjoy what you do or it will be harder to be successful.

7.5: How You Can Use This Information

Now that you have completed this chapter and made some difficult choices about whether to enter the workforce directly; enter the trades via an apprenticeship or technical school; enter military service; enter college to explore your options; or enter college with a set path to an identified career in your future … or some other nontraditional path, you are encouraged to move on to Chapter 8 where you will begin to explore ways to overcome any obstacles in the path to your chosen career.

7.6: Want More?

Don't forget that you have more opportunities to explore in the "Where to Turn" appendices at the end of this book, where you will find resources *In Print, On the Web,* and *On Campus.*

7.7: The Take Away

- Delayed gratification is not for everyone and the cost of college can be a burden for those who do not have a clear vision for attending. But conversely, many people discover their path while in college and enjoy the experience. This decision is a difficult one.

- A cost-benefit analysis of training and educational opportunities is nerve wracking, so get all your documents gathered and let your trusted others help you with these decisions. You don't have to do this alone.

References

Gardner, H. (2011). *Frames of mind: The theory of multiple intelligences.* New York: Basic Books.

Rosenbaum, J. E. (2001). *Beyond college for all: Career paths for the forgotten half.* New York: Russell Sage Foundation.

Ziglar, Z. (2007). *Better Than Good: Creating a Life You Can't Wait to Live.* New York: Thomas Nelson.

CONSIDERING YOUR CHALLENGES

WHAT IF YOU NEED HELP OR ACCOMMODATIONS TO SUCCEED?

You are welcomed here!

So far, I have spoken primarily about choices you will make, and I have been fairly positive in assuring you that these choices are in your control. I really do believe that, yet I am not so naïve as to ignore the challenges you might face, and I'm guessing you have been thinking about your challenges all along and wondering perhaps if there is some barrier in your path which makes you an exception to this process. Before you decide that perhaps this book isn't for you, can we take some time to look at the types of challenges you may be facing? I really do believe that you can cultivate the support you need to achieve your goals. Do you?

8.1: What We Know

A review of the literature tells us that a college education generally improves employment prospects (Carnevale, Smith, & Strohl, 2010), but sometimes there are perceived barriers to higher education. I say perceived, because some of the barriers you see on your path can be removed by professionals, programs, accommodations, and support. There is an old-school way of thinking that suggests that disability support is the responsibility of rehabilitation professionals, and academic support is the responsibility of faculty and their teaching assistants, and cultural minority support is the responsibility of the cultural community. However, I am happy to report that most campuses now provide collaborative services for academic success, career planning, and placement (Lee, 2004). In these collaborative designs, campus career counselors work closely with support professionals and faculty members to remove barriers and provide options for career success. In other words, you will not be facing your challenges alone.

8.2: How You Can Use This Information

It is hoped that you will take advantage of the myriad opportunities for support and accommodation that are in place, and that knowing these exist may help alleviate lingering anxiety from the resources discussion in Chapter 7. What you can do for yourself is to begin exploring the campus and community resources which can help bridge any perceived disadvantages or potential marginalization that is concerning you.

If you have a disability, then you probably already know that the Americans with Disabilities Act (ADA) makes it illegal for employers (with 15 or more employees) to discriminate on the basis of disability. What you may not know is that the ADA protection extends to your vocational training or higher education experiences as well. So whether you are headed straight into the workforce or to higher education, there are professionals in the community and on campus who can help you access accommodations for success. If you are seeking employment, your state division of vocational rehabilitation can help you understand your rights and accommodation needs. If you are seeking further education, each college/university will have, at a minimum, an ADA compliance officer, and many will have support services offices which provide diverse services for accommodation and success. Ask your school counselor (or your transition team if you have an IEP) to help you find the professionals and programs you will need after high school.

YOUR TURN 8.1

ADA Activity

Sometimes well-intentioned (?) prospective employers, faculty members, advisors, and others ask questions about your disability that are at best inappropriate and at worst illegal. With a trusted friend, family member, or counselor, role-play appropriately assertive responses to these inappropriate inquiries. Try not to let this list discourage you … you are unlikely to be asked all of these in your lifetime, but rehearsing your assertive responses can be empowering and can also keep you from becoming flustered if caught off guard with an inappropriate inquiry.

1. Do you have a disability?

2. What is your disability or diagnosis?

3. I know somebody else with your disability and that person didn't ask for this accommodation. Can't you just do it without all this fuss?

4. So you look "normal" to me. Is this some kind of mental illness?

5. Do other people in your family "suffer" from this same thing?

6. Are you going to be hospitalized all the time and miss work/absent from classes and expect everybody else to pick up the slack for you?

7. How did you get this disability?

8. Have you ever filed for worker's compensation? Sued an employer? Sued your school?

9. Did your parents/siblings do your work for you in the past, and do you expect your tutors/co-workers to do your work for you now?

10. If I give you an accommodation, that just gives you an edge over your classmates/co-workers. Why do you feel entitled to cheat your way to the top of the curve/top of the promotion race?

If you have had difficulty maintaining a high grade point average, or for other reasons believe that you would not be able to successfully navigate higher education, but are called to a career path that requires a college education, don't give up just yet. There are academic bridge programs at two- and four-year colleges that offer supplemental classes intended to bridge the gap between high school and college by providing supported learning, often in the areas of math, writing, reading comprehension, and study skills. Again, your high school counselor can help you find programs in your area, so don't give up on your dream if you think some help would make all the difference.

YOUR TURN 8.2

Academic Readiness Checklist

If you are wondering whether or not you are academically prepared for higher education, your high school transcript may not be enough to give you the answers you need. Sure, if you have a solid GPA with a good foundation in reading, writing, and math, you have a nice start. But sometimes it is your habits and tendencies that lead to success. If you can answer yes to most of the following statements, you are in a good place. If not, you might want to seek supportive academic coaching before you begin and during your first semester.

I like to read.

I like to use highlighters, notes, and tabs to make books my own.

I have read many good books and some that helped me think and reflect in a meaningful way.

I am open-minded and curious about ideas.

I like to encounter people with differing worldviews.

I am interested in becoming a better writer.

I look forward to discussing new ideas with both peers and faculty.

I know how to work deliberately to avoid procrastination and panic.

I am able to pace myself on projects and do not require anyone to micromanage my progress.

I ask others to give me feedback about my written drafts before I finalize and submit them.

I value collaboration.

I understand the value of being involved in my community.

I understand abstract mathematical and philosophical principles.

I brainstorm before I begin a new challenge.

I understand the difference between a quote and a paraphrase and I know how to cite each.

I am able to conduct library research on my own.

I always revise my work a number of times before I hand it in.

I am eager to engage with others and broaden my worldview.

I understand that listening is an important life skill and an essential college skill.

I value patience, empathy, personal generosity, and respect.

I have self-discipline, perseverance, and passion.

I know how to speak effectively in groups.

I understand why I need perseverance to finish my education.

I appreciate that my opportunity for further education should not be wasted.

I will not allow my newfound freedom to lead me away from my opportunity to reach my goals.

I will give back to my campus community.

Finally, if you consider yourself part of a potentially marginalized cultural group (LGBTQ+, English language learner, international student, person of color, and/or ethnic minority), you might be happy to know that many campuses are friendly and safer places for you to find your voice and your entry point to your desired career. Some of the better campuses have centers, programs, and student affairs professionals in place to help you transition from high school to college and then from college to the world of work or professional graduate programs while exploring the nuances of doing so as a member of a minority group. Your college counselor can help you explore these programs and find the best ones for you, and while you are at it, remember that there are also additional scholarships available to minority students.

YOUR TURN 8.3

Who Am I?

Sometimes seeking help on campuses or in the workplace means that we have to use labels … even if we are not ready to do so. Seeking support from LGBTQ+ services, the Asian-American center, the ADA compliance officer, or the advocate for students/employees of color can be a daunting task. Some of us embrace our labels with pride, and others would rather not be labeled.

To help prepare yourself to decide where you might identify with others in a meaningful way, try this activity. Write a poem entitled "Who Am I?" The only rule for your poem is that each line should begin with the words "I am …" It is entirely up to you if you prefer to use labels for aspects of your identity or if you prefer to use descriptive phrases that are open to interpretation. For example, a person could choose to say concretely "I am Canadian" or perhaps use stereotypes and say "I am from the land of maple leaves and maple syrup" or even a more abstract "I am safety in the north, land of wondrous waterfalls." This poem activity is completely up to your interpretation, but I hope you will consider including statements pertaining to your region of origin, ethnicity, religion/spirituality, ability, age/cohort, gender identity, critical memories from different points in your life, interests, hobbies, mottos/credos, favorite phrases, family traditions and customs, and whatever else may define an aspect of your lived experience and identity.

Reading back over your poem, where might you find connection and support on a campus or in the workplace?

8.3: How Can Professionals Help?

If you are facing any of the aforementioned challenges or other concerns that seem to be barriers along your path, I cannot stress enough that this would be a perfect reason to see a counseling professional in your school or in the community. Concerns about disability, physical health, emotional health, self-care, resources, academic or intellectual ability, gender and sexuality dialogues, language and culture differences, or any other potential source of marginalization can weigh heavily and convince you that your goals are out of reach. They are not. I repeat … THEY. ARE. NOT.

Counselors can help you to explore your differences and they can introduce you to tools and assessments, administered in person or online, which can help you recognize both your challenges and your strengths. Remember some of the strength-based positive psychology constructs we explored early in this book? Your counselor can assist you in using strength-based/ positive psychology and other measures that build confidence and help buffer against messages of marginalization. When you and your counselor begin discussing your strengths, you will see that they can outweigh your challenges and may help you to overcome the challenges … and hopefully embrace the aforementioned difference(s) as a source of strength, not a challenge at all.

8.4: How Others Use This Information

As in the previous chapters, two people have generously agreed to share this very personal aspect of their journeys with you, because they both believe that their stories will help you as you explore your unique challenges.

VOICES FROM CAMPUS 8.1

Kelsey's Corner (A Graduate Student's Perspective)

Let me start by saying the challenges I am about to talk about were almost completely brought on by myself. My last year of graduate school was one of the hardest years I have ever encountered in the 24 years of my life thus far. In my graduate program, the last year was the most demanding. As a graduate assistant, I was completing research projects and tying up loose ends with my professors before I left. As a student, I had to take the comprehensive exam to pass my program, pass the PRAXIS exam for state certification, apply for certification, apply for graduation, attend internship four days a week, and continue taking a full schedule of classes. Additionally, because I have high standards for myself, I also took an exam to make me a Nationally Certified Counselor. On top of that, I was continuing to pay my bills, recently engaged and planning a wedding, had just bought a house with my fiancé, and was applying for jobs. And as if all of THAT didn't seem like my plate overflowing, I convinced myself and my fiancé that it was the best time to adopt a puppy because … well puppies are adorable and stress relievers, right? See, this is what I was talking about earlier when I said I brought this on myself. Everything that was happening was extremely exciting, but it was stress. And believe it or not, good stress is still stress. It still taxes and impacts your body and thinking the same as bad stress. How did I make it through? Very carefully. Seriously, a lot of strategic time management and planning. Of course, school came first. I used every hour allotted in my graduate assistantship to complete my projects. And when I didn't have anything to do, I did homework or studied for one of the necessary exams. The other personal life stuff was planned around my school requirements. I had been with my then boyfriend for six years and I was not about to put a proposal on hold, so we planned the wedding for the fall after I graduated. Once we found the house we wanted, I specifically told my fiancé I could not go to settlement for the house until after I took the PRAXIS because I didn't want my head to be anywhere but counseling for the exam. Also I told myself we could not get a puppy until after I completed my comprehensive exam for my program which determined if I was going to graduate or not. In the end, it all worked out, but it would not have if I didn't have the skills and patience required for strict time management. In college, I worked in a research lab with doctoral students who mentored me. When I was worried about not finishing my thesis before graduation, one of them said, "It will get done, because it has to" and that is exactly right. Trust me, I wanted to procrastinate and focus on my wedding or play with my puppy every day, but my work had to get done. So it got done. And while I was completely mentally, physically, and emotionally drained by graduation, I got through it.

VOICES FROM CAMPUS 8.2

Rebekah's Voice (A New Professional's Perspective)

I already mentioned in previous chapters that I identify as a lesbian and I have a visual disability that legally prohibits me from driving. These are two identities that have caused me stress and anxiety during some points in my life.

In high school I struggled with my sexual orientation, and I come from a place where being part of the LGBTQ+ community wasn't really talked about. When I got to college I decided for myself I was done trying to hide who I was and wanted to embrace every aspect of myself. And that is exactly what I did. And I found that at my college, diversity for the most part was celebrated. I never really experienced harmful discrimination. Yes, some people are ignorant about differences, but that is going to be the case anywhere.

Also, in high school I had an Individual Education Plan (IEP) which allowed me the opportunity to sit down with my teachers at the beginning of the school year to discuss the accommodations I needed in their classrooms to be successful. This meeting was organized by the school, my parents, and the Intermediate Unit assigned to my school. When I got to college we had a Disability Support Services office, but they only provided me with documentation, stating that my professors had to accommodate me. Therefore, I had to email and meet with each professor individually. This was scary, but over time got easier. Some professors were happy to accommodate and some refused (although this is illegal). This was a turning point where I realized my disability might hold me back if some people felt my visual disability was my "problem."

When I was applying for jobs during my last semester of graduate school, I had many conversations with the Career Development Center about whether or not to come out as gay during my interview. Do I tell them about my visual disability during my interview? It's really up to you if you want to share identities during the interview process. I was lucky in terms of my sexual orientation as I applied for a job working with LGBTQ+ college students, so the assumption was already there, I just confirmed it in my interview. The idea of talking about my visual disability in my interview caused me great anxiety, mostly because I had a previous bad work experience.

I was able to work through how I'd share my disability without blatantly saying "Hey, I'm actually kind of blind." In higher education job searches, they bring you to campus for a day. I lived close to the campus, but a few days beforehand they offered to put me in a hotel the night before. On the phone I said "That'd be great as I do not drive." Over email they asked if I needed anything prior to my arrival. I told them if they plan to give me printed materials I'd like them in 18 pt. font. The day I was there I asked to use the ramps to go in and out of buildings. This gave them enough context clues to figure out I have a visual disability and guess what, I was offered the job!

Although sometimes our marginalized identities feel like faults or disadvantages, they can be really beneficial and help make you unique. I'm not saying I got my job because of my identities. I'm saying my identities play a role in my lived experience. And my lived experience, along with my education and resources, have helped me be successful. Some days are harder than others, but be proud of who you are—all of you!

8.5: How You Can Use This Information

Now that you have completed this chapter and hopefully decided that the bumps in your path just make the ride more exciting, you are encouraged to move on to Chapter 9 where you will begin to explore the process of readying yourself for the world of work. You will learn more about the documents and skills you will need. This may seem early for those of you considering more years of education at this point, but I encourage to continue anyway so that you can be intentional about the experiences you are cultivating now.

8.6: Want More?

Don't forget that you have more opportunities to explore in the "Where to Turn" appendices at the end of this book, where you will find resources *In Print, On the Web,* and *On Campus.*

8.7: The Take Away

- Challenges are only barriers if you allow them to be. You can choose to view them as opportunities for self-exploration and growth.

- Campus and community helping professionals are available to help you access the resources you need to overcome challenges in higher education and the world of work.

References

Carnevale, A. P., Smith, N., & Strohl, J. (2010). Help wanted: Projections of job and education requirements through 2018. Lumina Foundation.

Lee, C. (2004). Creating a collaborative campus culture. *Community College Journal of Research and Practice, 28*(6), 503–511.

UNIT III: ACTUALIZING YOUR CAREER: HOW DO YOU TRANSITION FROM DAYDREAM TO REALITY?

CHAPTER 9

DEMONSTRATING YOUR CAREER READINESS

HOW DO YOU PRESENT YOUR PROFESSIONAL SELF?

You only get one chance to make a first impression, so you'll want to get your ducks in a row to demonstrate your professional readiness to an employer.

Actualizing your career is a process that can be time consuming, frustrating, and oh so very rewarding. If you are ready (or getting ready) to seek a job (short-term goal) in line with your new career path (long-term goal), then this chapter will help you begin to transition from ideas to realities, by paying attention to how you present yourself professionally. This chapter will examine the documents you need to prepare and the interview situations you may want to consider in advance. Developing the skills to obtain a desired job is a process that will be useful for a lifetime.

9.1: What We Know

There is great debate in the literature right now about your Millennial generation and the ways in which your entry into the workforce will be different than the GenXers and Baby Boomers who preceded you. This is not the place to enter the debate, but I will remind you that, according to *Fortune*, you are part of the generation who "grew up in the shadow of September 11th and the Great Recession, and are well adapted to change, technologically savvy, and are poised to unleash innovation when given the right environment, support, and autonomy" (Lewis, 2015). But despite the unique paths that your generation is forging, the entryway to the workforce still requires getting all of your ducks and documents in a row to create an error-free résumé, write an interesting cover letter, and prepare to shine at your interview: Essentially the same advice I was given 35 years ago. But for you, I would like to add a caution about your documents. You are part of the digital native generation, which means that there is already an awful lot of information out there about you. Even if your résumé and cover letter are stellar, what will a potential employer find out about you if they Google your name? Think carefully about your social media accounts, and if necessary, clean them up. Remove tags on photos that are not consistent with your goals; delete statements that no longer reflect your thinking; disconnect from sites, pages, corporations, and individuals whose messages are not consistent with yours; and consider opening and creating a nice professional LinkedIn page to showcase you as a young up-and-coming professional.

9.2: How You Can Use This Information

I know this chapter can feel overwhelming, so let's break it down into three sections. Let's first explore résumé writing, then cover letters, and finally the interview process. These are the necessary 1,2,3s of the job search. I know that you might have already found work by walking into the right place at the right time or being connected by a family member or friend, but that will only help you find work, not necessarily a career.

Creating Your Résumé/Vita

If you have never drafted a résumé before, try not to panic. You may have heard that it is a listing of all of your jobs, and since you are just starting out, you might be wondering if yours will be very brief or even blank! The simple answer is, no. There are varying types of résumés (also called "briefs," "curriculum vitae," or "background information sheets"), and you can select a style and format that works for you, your experiences, and your chosen field. Remember that the goal of the résumé is to pave the way for an interview, so you'll want to select a style and descriptors that flatter you. Let's look at your format options.

Chronological: While this is the most common style, it is essentially a list of your employment history in reverse order (most recent on top) and requires that you have had job experiences (even if part-time or unpaid). If you are truly just starting out, this may not be best for you, even though it is popular.

Functional: This résumé style emphasizes skills instead of your employment history. If you are still in school and have not had a first job or two, this may be a better way to organize your first résumé. In a functional format, you can summarize the transferable skills that you bring from all of your experiences to the workplace.

Mixed Format: This style borrows from both functional and chronological styles and is the best of both worlds. However it can be a bit more stylistically complicated, so you might prefer to try a simple chronological or functional format first.

Most résumé formats begin with your name (not a nickname), mailing address, telephone number (whether you use your mobile number or a home number, check your outgoing message to be sure it is appropriate), email address (preferably using a form of your name, not something inappropriate for professional purposes), employment history if applicable, and educational background. Some résumé formats also allow for some optional information. There is great debate in the literature about which optional items are a good idea and which do not belong on a résumé. In order, from most often endorsed to often questionable, some additional options are job/career objectives, volunteer work, languages spoken/written, computer programs/technology skills, memberships in professional organizations, academic honors, references (only after obtaining their permission), hobbies, and personal information. If you need some help choosing a style and organizing your information, or if you want to see some sample résumés, there are many books and online resources dedicated to helping with the résumé writing process. You might want to start with resume-now.com.

As you draft your résumé, feel free to save multiple versions with differing objectives and optional components so you can choose and tailor the versions that seem most appropriate for each of your varying opportunities.

YOUR TURN 9.1

Résumé Starter Template

Here is one version of a basic résumé framework. Can you use it to create your first résumé or borrow from it to improve your existing draft?

Lucas Dresden
43 High School Road, Smalltown, DE 19700
voice/text: 302-555-5555
email: LDresden@gmail.com

EDUCATION

Smalltown High School, Smalltown, Delaware
2014 – 2018

WORK EXPERIENCE

Pet Sitter
2012 – Present
- Provided pet sitting services including dog walking, feeding, and yard care.

Childcare
2014 – Present
- Provided childcare for several families after school, weekends, and during vacations.

ACHIEVEMENTS

- National Honor Society: 2014, 2015, 2016
- Junior Class President: 2016–2017

VOLUNTEER EXPERIENCE

- Delaware Humane Association Dog Walker
- Delaware Special Olympics
- Smalltown Relay for Life

INTERESTS / ACTIVITIES

- Eagle Scout
- Swimming Team
- Drama Club

OTHER SKILLS

- Proficient with Microsoft Office Programs, Social Media Platforms, and Photo Editing
- Fluent in Spanish and Proficient in American Sign Language

Creating Your Cover Letter

Your cover letter (or letter of introduction/application) is a succinct business style correspondence which accompanies your résumé or application for a position. Though there is some debate about its importance in online applications, many experts agree that even résumés submitted via email should include a traditional cover letter rather than a simple email message. Ideally, the cover letter should include your address and the date, and it should be addressed to a specific person whenever possible. You should also check and double check the spelling of the individual's name and title. Though some older books or websites may still instruct you to open the letter with Dear Mr. Smith or Dear Ms. Smith, you will want to be cautious here. If you do not know for certain what an individual's gender identity and preferred title is, you should probably not try to guess whether Taylor Smith, Jordan Jones, or Pat Ling prefers Mr., Ms., Dr., Corporal, or the Reverend. Modern gender sensitive protocol suggests a more neutral "Dear Taylor Smith." Only if no individual name can be located should you resort to "Members of the Search Committee" or "To Whom It May Concern."

Next, your opening paragraph should state your purpose for writing: Is this a letter of introduction sent to an individual or organization expressing your general interest and/or a request for an informational interview? Or is this a response to an advertisement for a specific open position? Or perhaps you are sending your résumé as a follow-up to someone you have already spoken with on the phone or at a career fair? Make the reason for your contact clear in the first sentence or two.

Next, comes a larger paragraph where you will state the earliest date you are available for employment. This is particularly important if you are still a student. Then you can highlight just one or two points from your résumé, but you don't want to regurgitate the content of your résumé here, just a reinforcing comment or two. Rather than stating the same points in all of your cover letters, you might want to personalize this part and mention a skill or attribute which would best serve the organization you are contacting.

Your final paragraph is a request for consideration and an interview. You may want to put your telephone number and email here to facilitate that contact. And, while this may seem obvious, you will need to print this letter and place your signature above your typed name. Even if you are sending your documents electronically, you signature (traditional or electronic) is required.

YOUR TURN 9.2

Cover Letter Starter Template

Here is one version of a basic cover letter. Can you use it to create your first cover letter or borrow from it to improve your existing draft?

Julia Piper
4352 Baja Lane
Ocean Cliff, NJ 07855

April 9, 2018

Buffy Blue
Human Resources Coordinator
Forgotten Cats (Fundraising Division)
56 Main Street
Ocean Cliff, NJ 07855

Dear Ms. Blue:

This June, following my graduation from Ocean Cliff High School, I plan to pursue a summer position in fundraising before attending Monmouth University in the fall. I would like to explore possibilities with your agency.

It seems to me that I am always convincing folks to share their wealth with those in need. When I was a camp counselor, I persuaded a local art school to donate their surplus supplies so that I could start an art club with the older campers. I also convinced two students and one junior faculty member to donate some time to the club. I enjoyed this experience very much and believe that I will major in finance and social services, with a career goal of non-profit fundraising. But first, I would like to test this career direction with a summer of fundraising for Forgotten Cats.

Interestingly, I have recently learned that the best non-profit fundraisers are well organized, high energy, efficient individuals with a passion for the cause. I have all of these qualities, and a cat. As you can see, though my attached résumé is brief at this early stage, it reflects my early commitment to those in need and an emerging path toward fundraising, event planning, and leadership.

I hope my qualifications and aspirations interest you enough to pave the way for an interview. I would like to tell you more about myself and some promising ideas I have for Forgotten Cats fundraisers. I look forward to hearing from you (201-555-5555 voice/text or JPiper@gmail.com) at your earliest convenience. If I do not hear from you first, I will call the Forgotten Cats Office Coordinator, Lucas Bazinga, next week to see if a meeting can be arranged. Thank you for your time and consideration.

Sincerely,

(written signature here unless sending via email)

Julia Piper

Interview Considerations

If you have gotten to the interview stage, let me first offer you hearty con-gratulations. You must have done a great job with your cover letter and résumé. It's as if everything you have done since Chapter 1 (and even before we met) has been leading up to this moment. How nerve wracking, right? Okay just breathe. Let's break this down to three stages, what you should do before, during, and after your interview.

Before Your Interview

Ready? If you haven't already done so, now is the time to research your potential employer and, if possible, the person(s) interviewing you. Find out all you can about the mission, products, services, purpose of the organiza-tion and your interviwer(s)'s role there. No surprises right? You will want to respond to questions in a way that demonstrates your understanding. Next, you will want gather the materials you are bringing to the interview, such as copies of your résumé, work samples, list of references, and place them in a professional looking folder or portfolio. As the day of your interview approaches, you may want to practice positive self talk and remind yourself of all the reasons you would be excellent in this position. You may also want to remind yourself that the interview day may bring additional application forms to complete (so have a cheat sheet with dates, mailing addresses, and supervisors at previous positions), various tests, individual interviews, group interviews, meal interviews, and many, many questions. To help you prepare, you should organize your thoughts and practice your responses in advance.

YOUR TURN 9.3

Preparing for an Interview

It is never a good idea to go into an interview situation cold. Part of the process is to be calm, articulate, and well-spoken with your responses. If you have no idea what you want to say, you may freeze, respond awkwardly, or even avoid the question altogether with idle chatter. In preparation for interviewing, you may wish to respond to the following prompts, ether in a written journal format, in a conversation with a trusted other, or ideally, both.

1. You should be prepared to analyze your strengths and growth edges (what some people call weaknesses). You should be able to state your strengths with confidence and to share your growth edges as opportunities for development as you gain experience (not as problems for your potential employer). So … what is your greatest strength? And what is an area where you want to concentrate your growth efforts in the coming years?

2. How do you want to discuss the kinds of work you have already done? How can you speak about delivering newspapers, caring for children, serving food, stocking merchandise, or other beginning work opportunities in a way that highlights your accomplishments rather than demeans the experience? (Hint: no complaining about tasks, co-workers, or supervisors here. Keep it positive.) How can you speak about the endings of these early positions in a way that is developmentally appropriate? (Hint: speak about jobs ending because your after-school availability changed instead of saying "I quit.")

3. What would you like a potential employer to know about the skills you have acquired in early jobs? Through athletics, clubs, hobbies, and

leadership opportunities? Through responsibilities in your family or community? What skill(s) would you really like to sell?

4. What skills have you developed through formal education (high school and/or college) and other educational opportunities (tutoring? lessons? co-ops, apprenticeships? internships? 4H/scouts? camps?)

5. What special talents/gifts do you have? This isn't the time to be humble, so if you are musical, athletic, artistic, insightful, articulate, creative, or empathetic ... say so! And be prepared to say why you think these gifts can benefit your desired workplace.

6. What achievements have you made thus far? Again don't be shy and don't undersell yourself. If you helped raise $3,000 for a non-profit animal rescue, or if you helped clean up a local park after a storm because you value your community, or if you started your own lawn mowing business, tell your story and let the interviewer hear your compassion, pride, initiative, etc.

7. What are your general abilities and transferable skills? For example, are you an organizer? leader? problem solver? detail attender? big picture innovator? idea facilitator? team catalyst?

If you are really struggling with these questions, please talk to family, friends, teachers/professors, counselors, co-workers, coaches, mentors, advisors, supervisors, and anyone else who can give you a fresh perspective. Sometimes others see things in us that we don't see in ourselves until prompted.

Also, you will want to be cautious with your manner of dress. Even if the position will permit a casual dress or even provide a uniform, you will want to dress neatly and conservatively for your interview. There are many websites that provide guidance, though some styles are regional and pertain to certain industries and settings. If you are unsure, feel free to search online for photos of others who work there. Finally, it is imperative that you are punctual for your interview. If you are unfamiliar with the building, the drive, or the public transportation, you might want to do a trial run to be sure you know how long it will take to get there and then leave even earlier to be certain.

During the Interview

Most interview literature will advise you to be honest, and while I agree that honesty is important, you don't need to be brutally honest or divulge personal information that is not relevant or appropriate. For example, if an interviewer asks what your weaknesses are, it is appropriate to mention that you have growth edges and developmental milestones in your future such as becoming more appropriately assertive or finding a healthy work–life balance. It is not the time to start waxing poetic about your volatile temper, your excruciating IBS flare-ups, or your history of falling for romantic partners who cheat on you. In other words, know how much honesty is just too much information.

Do everything you can to demonstrate your interest in the position, the organization, and your interviewer. Listen carefully, show enthusiasm, take brief notes, and ask salient questions about the position, responsibilities, advancement opportunities, travel, hours, benefits, etc. Also, you will want to be as polite and positive as possible. This is not the time to cut people off in conversation, brag or exaggerate in an unpleasant way, or criticize former supervisors or employers. It is however the perfect time to relax, be yourself, express your sincere interest in the position, and close by asking when you can expect to hear from them and if you may check back to ask about the status of the position and whether or not you are still being considered.

After the Interview

It is still considered good form to send a handwritten thank-you note to your interviewer(s) and anyone else who was helpful, such as a human resources contact, an office administrative assistant, or an employee who showed you around. Though some modern sources will assert that it is completely acceptable to follow up with a thank-you email, the classic brief handwritten note is still the standard.

If time passes and you have not received a response by the agreed-upon date, you can call or write to ask about the status. And if you don't get the position? Well, you might want to ask if you can check back occasionally to find out about any new openings and to pleasantly express your continuing interest in employment. In other words, do not become rude, sullen, or dismissive if you are not chosen ... there is always a chance that the chosen candidate will not work out and/or that other opportunities will open up. Leave them thinking you are an excellent alternative.

But what if you are offered the job? Well then ... congratulations! Before you accept, carefully review the terms of your employment. Double check everything to make certain you understand your responsibilities, salary, benefits, hours, location, travel/transportation requirements, pace, working conditions, and opportunities for advancement. If it is what you want and you accept verbally, follow that up with a note or email confirming your start date and time (or appointment with human resources) and keep a copy in case there are any misunderstandings. Yay you!

9.4: How Others Use This Information | 122

9.3: How Can Professionals Help?

The wonderful thing about being part of a technologically savvy generation is that you probably know better than I what wonderful resources are available for free on the Internet. Résumé templates, cover letter samples, and even practice interview streams are there for you to use whenever you are ready to begin. That being said, your high school or college counselor can probably help you select resources that are best for your entry-level experience and career goals.

9.4: How Others Use This Information

Once again, our two fearless young adults have generously agreed to share with you, because they have spent many hours drafting, redrafting, changing, and tweaking their documents while wondering what the interview questions will be. They know how stressful this chapter must seem and they want you to know that it will be worth it when you get your employee ID card.

VOICES FROM CAMPUS 9.1

Kelsey's Corner (A Graduate Student's Perspective)

Oh, the joys of résumés, cover letters, and interviews. No, really, I mean it. They are so important and so valuable, regardless of how terrifying they are. I remember thinking in college as I was getting ready to apply to graduate school, "How is it fair that this little sheet of paper gets to determine my future?" and "How can I possibly sum up what my strengths are and all my experience on one page?" Résumés, cover letters, and interviews are so crucial to acquiring a job and entering your field of choice that my alma mater even made every single student enrolled in the university (around 40,000 students) take an English class specified to their field that legitimately taught us how to make and succeed at these. The truth is, there is not a single "correct" way to create a résumé. Yes, some have more curb appeal than others, but résumés are just as unique as you are. I mean, they are literally talking about everything YOU have done, not Suzy down the street. So is there really a wrong way to do it? That's what I had to tell myself so I would just finish my first draft. And oh, do I have so many drafts: separate résumés for school, for jobs, for a career, and for everything I have ever done. The worst thing I did was constantly compare my résumé content and format to every result found when I Googled "résumé formats." What I ended up creating from those searches wasn't what my field valued, and what my field valued on a résumé wasn't what my roommate's field valued so comparing was pointless. The best advice I have based on my own experience with the daunting tasks of résumés, cover letters, and interviews, even mock, is to just do it. Just sit down and create whatever *you* think your field values in a résumé. Then, put yourself out there; give your résumé or cover letter as practice to your professor, the career center, your roommate, or even your parents. Get the feedback everyone needs to just keep improving your already awesome self. Brainstorm potential interview questions, attend an actual mock interview, talk to yourself in the mirror, whatever it is, just do it. You will be so thankful you did when you need these skills for the real thing. I know I did. Even now, having obtained a real contract job in my field, I feel as though with every interview I attended (nine in total), I left feeling that I was better prepared for the next time. The truth is, you never stop learning with everything you do, so in fear of further sounding like a NIKE advertisement, just do it!

VOICES FROM CAMPUS 9.2

Rebekah's Voice (A New Professional's Perspective)

Although writing cover letters and revising your résumé can be time consuming, it's worth it! If an employer receives a cover letter that is generic, they won't look at your résumé. If your résumé has spelling errors in the first few lines, the employer may not continue to read it. I always viewed my cover letter as the hook, my résumé as the line, and my interview as the sinker. (Totally cliché, I know! But it's also true.) If your cover letter gets their attention, they will look at your résumé. If your résumé leaves them wanting to know more about you, they invite you to interview with them. It really is that simple.

Because you want your cover letter to be tailored to the job, that means you write a new one for every job. You can potentially keep parts of it like your contact information at the end, but otherwise this letter is expressing why YOU are the best for THIS job—not just A job. Use your resources to help you review your cover letters and résumés. These paper (or electronic) documents need to be the best they can be to get you to the interview (and hopefully the job).

When they say practice makes perfect, they are right. During my last year of graduate school I was given the opportunity to do mock interviews with professionals at my current university. I took advantage of that opportunity because I knew it would help me be more confident. I did an in-person mock interview and a phone mock interview. Each professional gave me valuable feedback. When I was called and offered a phone interview for my current job, I did THREE more mock phone interviews just for this one specific job. And it all paid off because the week after my phone interview I was called and invited to do an on-campus interview.

I'd also like to say a few words about dressing appropriately and conservatively. It is true that you should dress professionally. In addition, I want to emphasize wearing something that makes you feel confident! I don't know about you, but when I look good, I feel good. So I made sure my outfit helped me feel like I was on top of the world. With a positive attitude, feeling good, and my genuine excitement for the job, I can say it was all successful since the following week I was offered the job!

Lastly, I'd like to emphasize how important doing your research about the company can be. Some jobs require you do a presentation, and that requires knowing your audience. On many interviews they may ask "Why do you want to work for us?" or "What excites you most about working for our company?" They may even ask you what you know about the history of the company. I had to do a presentation for my interview, but even if I didn't need to do so, the information I learned on the university's website was very helpful to me.

Some of this may feel overwhelming, but just take a deep breath and take it moment by moment. I know you can do it.

9.5: How You Can Use This Information

Now that you have completed this chapter and have an idea of what you will need to land that first big job that kicks off your career, you are encouraged to move on to Chapter 10 where you will begin to explore your mentoring and networking opportunities, because you are not alone on your chosen path.

9.6: Want More?

Don't forget that you have more opportunities to explore in the "Where to Turn" appendices at the end of this book, where you will find resources *In Print, On the Web,* and *On Campus.*

9.7: The Take Away

- There is no one perfect résumé template, so within the appropriate guidelines, just breathe your unique style into a document (but even though it worked in *Legally Blonde*, I would avoid scented pink stationary!).

- •Make your interview mistakes while practicing with friends, laugh over it together, and then plan the better response for a real interview. In other words, don't allow that all-important interview to be your first interview.

References

Lewis, K. R. (2015, June 23). Everything you need to know about your millennial co-workers. *Fortune.* Retrieved from http://fortune.com/2015/06/23/know-your-millennial-co-workers/

CHAPTER 10

FINDING A MENTOR OR TWO

HOW DO YOU BEGIN CONNECTING AND NETWORKING?

"It's all about who you know."
Uhmmm … sometimes it really is!

There is little doubt that the best way to learn about a specific career is to talk to someone who is currently in your field of interest. What is even better is when that initial conversation grows into a mentoring relationship, where a more experienced individual takes an interest in your development and provides guidance along the journey. And while not every mentor can be a Mr. Miyagi or a Yoda, having others interested in your journey is a powerful asset.

10.1: What We Know

A review of the literature lets us know that mentoring can be effective in a variety of educational and professional settings. Most of the relationships studied appear to be more formalized relationships with intentional pairings, more formalized parameters and goals, and using systems to match mentors and mentees according to needs, interests, or other demographics. But the literature also suggests that informal mentoring relationships which occur spontaneously can be helpful. Sometimes informal mentoring can begin if you ask for help from someone more experienced, even if you don't come right out and ask that person to be your mentor. Informal mentoring can also occur when an existing relationship with a supervisor, educator, or peer morphs into a helping relationship. While either type of mentoring may be helpful to you at this point in your life, the literature does suggest that some of the best career development mentoring outcomes were derived from formalized and facilitated mentoring relationships which are structured to create effective change and growth in the mentee (Murray, 2001).

In addition to mentoring, you can also use your contacts for networking (finding out about opportunities and letting those with opportunities know about you). Though the concept of networking has its naysayers, the experts in the literature seem to agree that networking is the most effective way to find a job, with one source stating that "approximately 40 percent of all jobs are found this way" (Adams, 2011). Networking is a great way to find out about opportunities that are never advertised, which is why some people re-fer to networking as the hidden job market. Proponents of networking point out there are three benefits: access to information, access to resources, and career sponsorship (Seibert, Kraimer, & Liden, 2001).

10.2: How You Can Use This Information

So what can you do to find and build relationships with experienced individuals who may be willing to mentor you on this journey? You might choose to go straight to the experts themselves, the people who are actually involved in the types of careers that interest you. You can meet them at career fairs and alumni events, or if you are bold enough, you can contact folks directly and ask for an informational interview or even a shadowing day. You might also want to consider volunteering a few hours per week to assist someone in your field of interest, as more doors can sometimes open to potential mentors if you are not requiring a paycheck. If available in your school, on your campus, or in your community, sometimes joining clubs and teams can connect you to potential mentors as well. Finally, you can speak with a teacher/professor, school/campus counselor, librarian, or others in helping roles who may be able to connect you with an appropriate mentor and/or serve in that capacity for you.

YOUR TURN 10.1

Preparing to Approach a Potential Mentor

1. What type of mentor do you want or need? A professional in your chosen field for career-related guidance? A supportive helper to encourage you and provide space to discuss your future? A coach to challenge you and help you push through any fears and periods of procrastination? All of the above? List a few possibilities here:

   _____

   _____

   _____

   _____

   _____

2. How do you like to communicate? Are you willing to sit down face to face over coffee (or via Skype) with a mentor and set aside some quality time to spend with this person to develop on ongoing longer term relationship? Or are you looking more for a resource—someone to answer your questions via email, text, and/or brief casual interactions? It is important to be clear about what you want and to communicate those expectations to a potential mentor. Take a moment to describe the interaction you are seeking:

_____

_____

_____

_____

_____

3. What are you going to say? Remember that you are initiating this relationship and so you will be expected to take the lead and set a healthy mutually respectful tone to your interactions. Consider the following checklist before your first meeting:

- Have you scheduled a time/place that will allow you to be punctual?

- Have you considered what dress is appropriate for the meeting, especially if you are meeting your new mentor in a professional setting or place of employment?

- Do your cultural expectations match those of your new mentor? Have you considered whether you will shake hands? bow slightly? smile and nod? pick up the check if meeting for coffee? send a thank-you note after the first meeting?

- Have you prepared a few questions to facilitate the conversation, especially if you might be nervous?

- Have you brought a watch or your SILENCED mobile phone so you can watch the time and not overstay your welcome (30–60 minutes is generally the expected meeting time unless you have agreed otherwise)?

- If you plan to use your mentors for networking, you might want to be prepared to ask if there are other people they might be willing to help you contact to increase your opportunities. To prepare for this discussion, you might want to have simple "business cards" made with your name and contact information. You can leave a few of these with your mentors and ask for theirs in return if applicable.

Some of those same people you are selecting as mentors can also be used to begin your network of contacts. Your network will continue to grow from there as it consists of the people you know and the people they know. So for example, if you tell someone that you are looking for a certain type of opportunity, that person may not have answers but may mention it to a colleague who just heard about an opening from a relative. The information about the position flows back to you and, if you are lucky, your name is also given to the potential employer and a connection is made. When you network, you develop the ability to build and maintain relationships with an extended circle of people, which helps with your job search and can also be a key to success in your long-term career.

YOUR TURN 10.2

Sample Questions for Networking via a
Career-Based Informational Interview

The following questions can be helpful when you have the opportunity to meet a professional in your field of interest for an informational interview as part of your networking process. Why not practice now by interviewing family members or other volunteers about their careers?

1. How much training or formal education is required to enter your field? Does it require a college degree, graduate/professional degree, certification/licensure, specialized training, or apprenticeship?

2. In your opinion, what kinds of work experiences, activities, or college majors would provide a good background to enter your field?

3. What specific personal qualities are important in your field?

4. What is a typical entry-level position in your field?

5. Do you know how competitive the job market is at the entry level in your field? Is that just in this area or all over the United States? Other countries?

6. What is the typical career path for someone in your field?

7. How did you enter this field?

8. Will you summarize a typical day, week, month for me?

9. How are your responsibilities determined? Do you set your own schedule? Do you have opportunities to work autonomously on tasks that you determine to be important?

10. What are the best and worst parts of your job?

11. How long have you been in your field and how greatly have your job descriptions changed (or will change) as you advance?

12. Can you describe the organizational structures in your field? To whom do you report and do others report to you?

13. Do you generally work alone or do you have frequent contact with others (co-workers, clients, the public)?

14. What do you find personally rewarding or fulfilling about your work?

15. If you were starting over again, would you plan your career the same way? What would you do differently?

16. How many hours per week do you generally spend at your place of work? Do you often put in extra time from home? Are you required to work nights, weekends, holidays, or "overtime" shifts?

17. Does your position require travel? How often and how far and are expenses covered?

18. What is the average starting salary for a position in your field? And the approximate highest salary potential?

19. How much flexibility do you have in terms of responsibilities, duties, hours, dress, etc.?

20. The work you are doing now, will you make it your life's career or will you go in another direction from here?

21. What other occupations are closely related to what you do?

22. What is the future of your field? Do you see new and expanding opportunities?

23. How can I find out more about your field? What is the best way to break into the profession?

24. Can you suggest other individuals or organizations who may be able to provide me with additional information?

25. Do you have any other insights which might help me? Is there anything we did not discuss which you think would be helpful for me to know?

10.3: How Can Professionals Help?

Finding mentors and beginning to network may feel quite intimidating, especially if you have a great deal of introverted energy and prefer fewer people in your circles. If you are not feeling ready to jump in and cultivate these early relationships for yourself, perhaps your school counselor or college placement office can help you connect with a formalized program for mentoring and/or networking. These programs often use volunteers and alumni who are excited to pay it forward, so it might make the process less awkward at first, knowing that they really do want to help you.

10.4: How Others Use This Information

Mentoring and networking helped the two people who write your campus voices essays and they were happy to share this process with you as well.

VOICES FROM CAMPUS 10.1

Kelsey's Corner (A Graduate Student's Perspective)

If you speak to anyone who has been through college or dove right into their career, you are probably going to find a common theme or piece of advice: networking. It was engrained in my head from day one receiving tours at college campuses—"Network all you can, and you will have a better chance of getting a job." Now did I believe this? No. If you take the same classes as your friend who is in the same major as you and you get the same grades, then you should have the same likelihood of getting a job, right? Not necessarily. But the truth is, networking doesn't just occur at college or in professional settings, you could network anywhere. Little did I know, I had been networking since high school. To me, networking is just building a positive relationship that can be transferred to a professional setting. I had been building relationships my whole life and lucky for me, I wanted to work in the education system where I had been for 18 years of my life. I didn't know it then, but one of the relationships I built as a high school student would be one of the best networks I would ever have while pursuing a career in school counseling. I frequently visited my school counselor in high school because I was a teenage girl who lived in drama. Then, my counselor was my confidant, someone who would be able to talk down my anxiety attacks and listen to me talk about how my parents just don't understand. I was too self-centered then to realize that I was learning so much more from him, even if it wouldn't truly be put into use until graduate school. After graduating from high school, I had made such a meaningful relationship with my counselor that he told me to keep in touch, which is sometimes a meaningless thing people say to each other when you know you'll probably never see them again. Well, I did keep in touch. Only briefly, about once a year, but that kept my network strong while I was transforming into a professional myself. Fast-forward to my first year of graduate school. I was looking for an internship as a school counselor and, lo and behold, my high school counselor came through. Turns out he had become a principal and through a truly crazy series of twists and turns, he got me an internship at his new school with one of his counselors. Not only did I gain experience from that network but he also wrote me a fantastic letter of recommendation speaking as a counselor as well as a principal. Here I am, 10 years after meeting my high school counselor and I have a career in the field I love so dearly in part because my current principal valued his opinion as a reference as another principal. Now, my circumstance is my own and yours may be different, but the tour guides aren't lying. Networking could realistically get you a job someday.

VOICES FROM CAMPUS 10.2

Rebekah's Voice (A New Professional's Perspective)

People will sometimes say, "It's not what you know, it's who you know." I partially believe this statement. I'd rather say "It's who you know AND what you know." You probably won't be given a job just because you know the boss's brother, but you might get the boss to give you an interview because you know the boss's brother. Follow me? Mentors are a very important part of a person's career journey. Remember I spoke about my "Aha!" moment in Chapter 5? That moment occurred because I took the time to reach out to my mentor and ask for help. She provided me insight and helped me to be successful.

The funny thing is, my mentor used to work at the same university where I work now. She provided me with information about this position and she served as a reference as well. When I sat down in one of my interviews (with an all-day-long on-campus interview you meet with multiple people at different times), the first thing the person across the table from me said after his name and it's nice to meet you was, "So how do you know *mentors name here*?" And honestly, it gave me some relief because he is in a prestigious position at the university, yet this felt more like a casual conversation than an interview, because we had a common contact. I told him how I knew her, he continued with some other important questions, and I felt more confident because we had a connection. And an even funnier thing is, he is now a mentor to me, too!

One important thing to remember about networking and mentorship is not only about what you GET from the relationship, but also about what you can GIVE. You may think you don't have anything to give, but you do. The networking and mentoring relationships you create need to be genuine and not feel forced or like you are only part of it to get something from it. It's human nature to have relationships; networking relationships are just more strategic sometimes. Maybe you can even think about some relationships you have already formed with people. Could any of those become networking or mentoring relationships? I bet you can think of at least one. It's usually true that you will not find what you want unless you look for it.

10.5: How You Can Use This Information

Now that you have completed this chapter and found a mentor or two who can help you network and move forward on your chosen path, you are encouraged to move on to Chapter 11 (the final chapter) where you will finish your early career path exploration by considering ways to stay the course through difficult times and not lose sight of your longer term goals.

10.6: Want More?

Don't forget that you have more opportunities to explore in the "Where to Turn" appendices at the end of this book, where you will find resources *In Print, On the Web,* and *On Campus.*

10.7: The Take Away

- Mentors are individuals who are farther along their career paths and care about yours. You need one (or more). Find a good candidate and respectfully cultivate that relationship.

- The term networking is overused for a very good reason. People who network are in the know and connected in ways that lead to success. Never consider networking a waste of time.

References

Adams, S. (2011, June 7). Networking is still the best way to find a job, survey says. *Forbes.* Retrieved from https://www.forbes.com/sites/susanadams/2011/06/07/networking-is-still-the-best-way-to-find-a-job-survey-says/#4f16f7af4366

Murray, M. (2001). *Beyond the myths and magic of mentoring: How to facilitate an effective mentoring process.* San Francisco: Jossey-Bass.

Seibert, S. E., Kraimer, M. L., & Liden, R. C. (2001). A social capital theory of career success. *Academy of Management Journal, 44*(2), 219–237.

STAYING THE COURSE

WHAT IS YOUR LONG-TERM PLAN?

People like to cherry-pick the parts of their career that they're either in the midst of or that they're the most proud of, but the truth is careers and lives are tapestries.

—Mike Rowe

So here we are at the end of our time together. Hopefully you now have a completed puzzle which shows a picture of your potential future—one made of pieces of yourself, your world, the choices you have made, and what you have learned thus far. If you have come to discover that you want more than just a job with a paycheck and that you are ready to plan a career that will be a key to getting what you want and need for many years to come, then this final chapter is a launching pad and a farewell. I hope that you will use these final suggestions as you make more concrete plans for your future.

11.1: What We Know

The literature supports the idea that a carefully chosen long-term career path is often more successful than a path of least resistance, jumping from easy opportunity to easy opportunity. At this point, you have assessed your interests, skills, resources, and opportunities and have begun readying yourself for a career that fits. I don't know if you have chosen higher education, graduate/professional education, the trades/apprenticeships, an entrepreneurial opportunity, a family business, military service, or one of many other nontraditional routes; but I do know that all are viable options and you have chosen for your own reasons. I commend you for having a plan that works for you and your unique set of parameters. Looking to the future, I want to end with a brief look at the literature pertaining to staying the course on longer journeys with the inevitable delayed gratification. The good news for your generation is that new concepts of boundaryless careers are replacing the old views of linear, lifespan careers with traditional ways of measuring success (Eby, Butts, & Lockwood, 2003). In these new systems, young people are achieving career success by knowing themselves, setting realistic expectations for personal growth, and developing positive relationships, including the skill of networking. These are all things you have been doing with this book, so you are well positioned for success.

Finally, you might just be wondering, what if things don't work out? What if you find yourself unhappy, unfulfilled, or financially compromised by your choices? Well, remember that this is a journey not a destination. There is plenty of information out there, in print, on the Web, or with a counselor that can help you can fine-tune your choices, re-direct your energy, revert to the last choice that felt right, make a dramatic mid-life change, and/or cope with unexpected derailments.

11.2: How You Can Use This Information

As you head down the career path you have chosen, I'd like to offer some final advice if you are willing to read just a bit more. First and foremost, please be realistic about your expectations and patient about your progress. No job, no career is perfect. You will experience frustration and setbacks. We all do. Try to use the positive aspects of your career to help you weather the storms … because there will be storms. They are inevitable. But you are stronger than bad weather, and calm seas with growth opportunities are right around the bend.

Be proactive and show initiative, always doing more than your minimum basic expectations. If you see something that needs to be done or a policy/ procedure that could be improved, step up and ask about accepting responsibility for those changes. Offer to help, offer to lead, offer to join a team, offer to demonstrate that you leave things better than you found them.

As you work with others, remember that your work habits and reflexive responses have a domino effect. Make efforts to be cooperative, considerate, conscientious, and mature. Embrace your role as part of the team, and respect that team by being punctual, flexible, and respectful while controlling your emotional responses and considering the system goals. If this isn't easy or natural for you, consider working with a mentor to fine-tune these professional growth edges.

Finally, what if you realize that the choices you have made are no longer feeling like a calling, but perhaps a burden, a mismatch, or even a mistake? Well, you are not alone and you have the ability to back up to the last intersection where it still felt right and correct your choice. Many people veer down side paths and some just start fresh. Gather the experiences, new transferable skills, professional growth, letters of reference, new understanding of yourself … and start again! Your career calling is a journey, not an end goal. Onward and upward!

YOUR TURN 11.1

A Friday Morning in 2040

This is the final activity in this book. If you like to write, you can journal your response, but most people prefer to audio record their responses or speak to a trusted other.

Close your eyes and imagine a Friday morning in the year 2040. You are just waking up _____(alone? with someone else? pet?). You open your eyes and you see _____. The air is _____? Through the window, it is _____? You feel _____? You look over to see your clothes for the day and they are _____? You look at the clock and see the time is _____ and you don't have to be _____ until _____?

Now continue on. Tell us about your day, your life, your work, your people, your emotions. Describe this day. Now hold onto it when the journey gets rocky. This! This is what you are working toward.

11.3: How Can Professionals Help?

If you find yourself struggling at any point in your career, remember that you are not alone. Many educational institutions offer lifetime career planning and placement services to their alumni. Additionally, there are counselors in the community that you can access if you want help. And of course, I imagine in our technologically advancing society, that years down the road, you will probably be even more likely to seek assistance from resources online or via an app. I can't predict where we will all be in 20 years, or if I will still be on the journey myself, but I know for sure that help will be available to you if you want it.

11.4: How Others Use This Information

As we close out this book, your essay writers are sending you forward with some final words of wisdom and experience.

VOICES FROM CAMPUS 11.1

Kelsey's Corner (A Graduate Student's Perspective)

As you begin to consider and plan your career or education journey, I am in the middle of mine. I have just completed six years of education needed for my desired career. I have also just accepted a contract position in a school district, literally three weeks after graduating. Crazy right? To me it is because I never thought I would get here. It is so very important to remember that it will be tough in at least one way or the other, but it will be fantastic. If you expect there to be bumps along the way, it won't be as hard when you hit them. Over my six years of education, particularly in the final two years of graduate school, the amount of times I felt completely overwhelmed and like it was never going to end are too many to count. At the ages of 23 and 24, I was still calling my mom crying because I didn't know if I could do it. After all that time, all the highs and all the lows,

I have reached my career goal and now I start my new journey as a professional school counselor. If you are passionate about what you are doing and learning about, do not give up. Understand? Do. Not. Give. Up. It will be the most rewarding feeling when you reach the end and can look back and say "I did this. I did all of this." My good friends from graduate school and I have a joke that we can smile and laugh about fondly now: If you don't have a breakdown during graduate school, did you actually go to graduate school? Now this was our specific reality, and yours may be different, but the point is, we made it and we made it together. Look for the support systems, the networks, the friends, and the fellow students or co-workers who are going through the same thing. It is comforting to know that you are not alone on this career journey. Before I leave you, there is one last thing I want to tell you about. There is a song I listened to by the band OK Go throughout college and graduate school that resonated with me when I was struggling; the chorus was simply, "Let it go, this too shall pass." Now that I am in the professional world and can look back on my journey to this point, nothing has ever been truer to me. The last 11 chapters were my story. Now go, spend time molding your journey into what you want it to be. Take time to laugh, breathe, and allow yourself to binge watch a TV series every once in a while. And above all, enjoy the process, you are creating your own story, after all.

VOICES FROM CAMPUS 11.2

Rebekah's Voice (A New Professional's Perspective)

I've been at my first professional job for two years now and when I started my graduate work, this was my dream job. Sometimes people think a dream is called a dream because it's unattainable. I call a dream a dream because dreams can come true! Your dream job can become a reality if you work for it. No one is going to come up to you and hand you an envelope with an offer letter to your dream job if you aren't putting in any effort.

And maybe your first job isn't your dream job and that's okay too; but, it could be a good starting point to give you great skills and experiences in order to be a better applicant for your dream job. Or maybe your dream job isn't what you thought it would be. Or turns out it isn't your dream job after all. All of these scenarios are possibilities. Your job will change. Your career may even change over time because that's how life works. Staying positive is the best way to continue to move forward.

Even as a professional, I don't have all the answers (imagine that!) and I still need to ask for help sometimes. My mentors often come in handy! Some days everything still feels overwhelming and I just take a deep breath and take it moment by moment. Some days are harder than others and that will always be the case. I have to trust myself just like you have to trust yourself. You know what is right for you.

As I was writing my story for each chapter, I kept thinking how much I wish I had this book when I was struggling with my career and job decisions. You are lucky to have such a great resource available to you. I hope you've enjoyed reading my story as much as I've enjoyed sharing it with you. While you continue to think about and explore your career path, remember this book only gave you two perspectives. Maybe one of them resonated with you, but if one of them didn't, feel free to reach out to others you know and have them share their story with you. Every person has their own story and I'm excited to know you're starting to write yours!

11.5: How You Can Use This Information

Now that you have completed this chapter and this book, you have outlined a path for yourself. I want to end by reminding you that at ANY time you can go back to ANY chapter and step through it again making adjustments. I will however caution you of the ripple effect … if you make a large change to your responses in any one chapter, you may want to consider how that change impacts your responses in other chapters.

11.6: Want More?

Don't forget that you have more opportunities to explore in the "Where to Turn" appendices at the end of this book, where you will find resources *In Print, On the Web,* and *On Campus.*

11.7: The Take Away

- You have all the tools you need to be successful, so start actualizing that career dream now.
- •Take a deep breath, take a first step … you got this!

References

Eby, L. T., Butts, M., & Lockwood, A. (2003). Predictors of success in the era of the boundaryless career. *Journal of Organizational Behavior, 24,* 689–708. doi:10.1002/job.214

Rowe, M. (2009, October 7). The real dirt on Mike Rowe of 'Dirty Jobs.' *Entertainment Weekly Online.* Retrieved from http://ew.com/article/2009/10/07/the-real-dirt-on-mike-rowe-of-dirty-jobs/

APPENDIX

WHERE TO TURN—
ADDITIONAL RESOURCES

In Print

Bell, A. H., & Smith, D. M. (2004). *Interviewing for Success*. NJ: Pearson Prentice Hall.

Boldt, L. G. (2009). *Zen and the Art of Making a Living: A Practical Guide to Creative Career Design* (Rev. ed.). New York, NY: Penguin Books.

Bolles, R. N. (2017). *What Color is Your Parachute?: A Practical Manual for Job-Hunters and Career-Changers7*. Berkeley, CA: Ten Speed Press.

Brooks, K. (2009). *You Majored in What?: Mapping Your Path From Chaos to Career*. New York, NY: Viking.

Fogg, N., Harrington, P., & Harrington, T. F. (2012). *College Majors Handbook With Real Career Paths and Payoffs: The Actual Jobs, Earnings, and Trends for Graduates of 60 College Majors* (3rd ed.). Indianapolis, IN: JIST Works.

Levoy, G. (1997). *Callings: Finding and Following an Authentic Life*. New York, NY: Harmony Books.

Rosenbaum, J. E. (2001). *Beyond College for All: Career Paths for the Forgotten Half*. New York, NY: Russell Sage Foundation.

Tieger, P. D., & Barron-Tieger, B. (2007). *Do What You Are: Discover the Perfect Career for You Through the Secrets of Personality Type* (4th ed.). New York, NY: Little, Brown.

On the Web

AIFS Study Abroad
https://www.aifsabroad.com/

ASVAB Career Exploration Program
http://www.asvabprogram.com/

Bureau of Labor Statistics—Occupational Outlook Handbook
http://www.bls.gov/oco/

Career Opportunities for Students With Disabilities
http://www.cosdonline.org/

Careers.org
http://www.careers.org/

CareerBuilder
http://www.careerbuilder.com/

CareerJet
https://www.careerjet.com/

CareerOneStop
https://www.careeronestop.org/

College Affordability and Transparency Center
https://collegecost.ed.gov/catc/

College Navigator
https://nces.ed.gov/collegenavigator/

Coolworks—Jobs in Great Places
https://www.coolworks.com/

Corporate Equality Index
http://www.hrc.org/campaigns/corporate-equality-index

Diversity Employers
http://www.iminorities.com/

Educate to Career
https://www.jobsearchintelligence.com/salary-calculator-intro-etc

ExPat Network
https://www.expatnetwork.com/

Federal Internships
http://www.dcjobsource.com/fedinterns.html

Feds Hire Vets
https://www.fedshirevets.gov/index.aspx

Glassdoor
https://www.glassdoor.com/index.htm

Goodwill Community Foundation (Learn Free)
https://www.gcflearnfree.org/subjects/career/

Go Abroad
https://www.goabroad.com/

GradSense
http://gradsense.org/gradsense

Idealist
https://www.idealist.org/

Indeed
https://www.indeed.com/

Interviewing Software
http://interviewingsoftware.com/free-video-interviews/

Job Accommodation Network
https://askjan.org/

Job Corps
https://www.jobcorps.gov/home.aspx

Job-Hunt
https://www.job-hunt.org/

Jobster
http://jobster.com/

Learn How to Become
http://www.learnhowtobecome.org/

LinkedIn
http://www.linkedin.com/

LinkUp
http://www.linkup.com/

MAPP Your True Calling
http://www.assessment.com/

Millennial Workplace Expert—Lindsey Pollak (blog)
https://www.lindseypollak.com/blog/

Monster
http://www.monster.com/

My Interview Simulator
http://myinterviewsimulator.com/

National Institute for Women in Trades, Technology and Science
http://www.iwitts.org/

O*Net
http://online.onetcenter.org/

Oodle Jobs
http://jobs.oodle.com/

Out & Equal LGBT Career Link
http://outandequal.org/lgbt-careerlink/

Payscale Salary Negotiation Guide
http://www.payscale.com/salary-negotiation-guide

Peace Corps
https://www.peacecorps.gov/volunteer/volunteer-openings/

Peterson's Guides
https://www.petersons.com/

Public Service Careers
http://publicservicecareers.org/

Quintessential Careers
https://www.livecareer.com/quintessential

Raw Resume
http://www.rawresume.com/

Resume Writing Academy
http://www.resumewritingacademy.com/

Salary.com
http://salary.com/category/salary/

SREB Academic Common Market
https://www.sreb.org/academic-common-market

Talent Zoo
http://www.talentzoo.com/

The Smart Student Guide to Financial id
http://www.finaid.org/ http://www.finaid.org/

USA Jobs
https://www.usajobs.gov/

USDE College Score Card
https://collegescorecard.ed.gov/

USDE Federal Student Aid
https://studentaid.ed.gov/sa/

Vault
http://www.vault.com/

WetFeet
http://www.wetfeet.com

Workforce Recruitment Program
https://wrp.gov/AboutPre.do

On Campus

Counseling Services
Academic Advising Services
Career Planning Services
Placement Services
Disability Support Services
Multicultural Support Services
LGBTQ Support Services
Financial Aid Services
Alumni Services
Dean of Students
Director of Student Services
Faculty Members
Peers